"The CEO's Guide to The Diversity, Equity & Inclusion Culture Journey".

TOP DOWN COMMITMENT

How Good CEOs Do Diversity and Great Ones Build Culture

PRAISE FOR
"Top Down Commitment"

This book can make a real difference for leaders.

"Jocelyn Giangrande's clarity of thought and pragmatic approach jumps off the page as she guides us through the steps required to instill a DEI culture. She builds on the pillars of effective management to show us how DEI can further our organizational goals when it becomes an intrinsic and visible value. This book has long been needed, yet it couldn't be more timely or relevant. Although written for CEOs, every high-performing team (or any team that aspires to be high performing) should read this book and follow its brilliant playbook."

    - DAVID GREENE, President Colby College

"Being a builder is at the core of any successful CEO, leader, or business owner. We build companies, brands, and teams, but it doesn't matter if we don't first build a culture that is rooted in DEI. Every builder needs an architect, and Jocelyn understands what it takes to build diverse, equitable, and inclusive teams.

    - TONY COLES, Division President, iHeartMedia
    Black Information Network (BIN)

"In print, Jocelyn Giangrande is just as direct and thoughtful as she is in person. *Top-Down Commitment, How Good CEOs Do Diversity and Great Ones Build Culture* provides common-sense direction and a clear process for driving an inclusive, respectful, and fair culture. For those that are tempted to think of DEI as checking boxes, she clearly warns that we must be both diligent and patient and that it is "...employee morale, having all voices heard, total engagement, removing barriers to ensure a level playing field and treating people with respect and dignity that are the true measures of a DEI culture."

    - MICHAEL GOAD, President, Dow Chemical Employee Credit Union

"A commitment to diversity involves everyone and all represented groups in an organization. As an organization expands its employee base, and especially if it is a global company, the need for cultural awareness throughout the organization becomes essential to managing."

"In the current fierce competition for talent, it's essential that organizations tap all sources of employees. Doing so mean reaching into diverse populations that may not have been considered or are not part of the organization's existing network. To be successful, a commitment to diversity and cultural awareness is essential to make sure employees from all represented groups are supported, productive, and committed to the organization."

    - BRAD COULTER, President & CEO, Matrix Human Services

"Jocelyn's book, *Top-Down Commitment: How Good CEOs Do Diversity and How Great Ones Build Culture* is an essential read for any leader in an organization. It is a practical and timely read and a valuable resource for CEOs and all leaders that want to be at the forefront of building a superior DEI culture. Jocelyn writes in an easy, straightforward style and provides easy to understand steps to develop a structured, thorough DEI plan for the workplace. The book is laid out with challenges built in along the way. It provides a solid roadmap for developing a great DEI program with a lesson in each of the 10 chapters."

- MARY E. CORRADO, President and CEO, ASE

This book truly distinguishes itself from so many other DEI books because of its straight talk to CEOs and the practical and actionable guidance that it provides.

In *Top-Down Commitment*, Jocelyn Giangrande delivers straight talk to CEOs about their critical role in building, leading, and sustaining a culture that is diverse, equitable and inclusive. She addresses the challenges and provides practical and actionable guidance on how to ignite the change and engage top leaders on the journey. This book is a well-documented, authoritative source for today's top leaders who are ready to take their companies to the next level of excellence.

- MONICA E. EMERSON, Former U.S. Department of the Navy, Diversity Officer; Retired Daimler Chrysler, Corporate Diversity Officer, Founder and Principal, Inclusive Performance Solutions

"Jocelyn Giangrande shares her many talents, expertise, and experience with focus on insight, strategy, process, and presence in her thoughtful resource in the lifelong learning journey about effectiveness in creating inclusive cultures. She writes pragmatically with the "must dos" for corporate leaders and the consultants that advise them. She explores the "why" of foundational work for today's organizations to succeed in the human performance sphere of diversity, equity, and inclusion. It is a valuable addition to understanding our imperative in creating great places to work."

- LAURITA THOMAS, President, American Research Universities - Human Resources Institute

"Let Jocelyn be your guide on your personalized DEI journey. Follow her action steps for a realistic and positive approach. With Jocelyn's direction you will develop, communicate, measure, and successfully implement your own customized business plan. I appreciated learning how to integrate and incorporate DEI into my every-day business practices. Start today, "Be a Great One" and make a difference in your business, your community, and our world."

- JULIE A. MCFARLAND, President, McNaughton & Gunn

"The CEO's Guide to The Diversity, Equity & Inclusion Culture Journey".

TOP DOWN COMMITMENT

How Good CEOs Do Diversity and Great Ones Build Culture

JOCELYN GIANGRANDE

SASHE LLC · BLOOMFIELD, MICHIGAN

Top Down Commitment: How Good CEOs Do Diversity
and Great Ones Build Culture

©2022 Jocelyn Giangrande
SASHE, LLC • Bloomfield, Michigan

ISBN: 978-0-9839816-5-7
Library of Congress Control Number: 2022916767

Published by SASHE, LLC • Bloomfield, MI 48304
www.jocelyngiangrande.com

CREDITS
Editor: Tenita C. Johnson, So It Is Written, LLC
Cover and Interior Design: LaTanya Orr, Selah Branding and Design LLC
Author Photo: Shaleena Cole

Printed in the United States of America.

DEDICATION

This book is dedicated to all my clients who invited me
into their organizations and trusted me to accompany, partner,
and guide them on their DEI cultural journeys...

and

to you,

The Great CEO,
ready to commit from the top down!

ACKNOWLEDGEMENTS

This book could not have happened without the support, encouragement and listening ear of my mother and best friend. She spent countless hours reading this book, listening to my ideas, thoughts and concerns, and helping me sort through approaches.Her patience and confidence, along with our candid conversations about DEI, helped take this book from a dream to reality.

My clients, friends, mentors, experts and peers who do this work also deserve acknowledgment. Because of their trust, support, contributions and openness, I learn and grow every day.

The great leaders, Nancy Schlichting and Mark Gray, who both helped set the tone for this book are acknowledged. Through their top-down commitment, they stepped apart from the good and joined the great. Most importantly, for their commitment to build diverse, equitable and inclusive organizations.

I would also like to acknowledge my longtime friend, LaTanya Orr, who is responsible for the layout, cover design and graphics. I'd like to thank the editor, Tenita Johnson, founder of "So It Is Written". It takes relationships like these to make a dream reality.

The CEOs who read this book also deserve acknowledgment. I am grateful for their top-down commitment.

Lastly, I must acknowledge my husband and son for their support. They are the muse for my work.

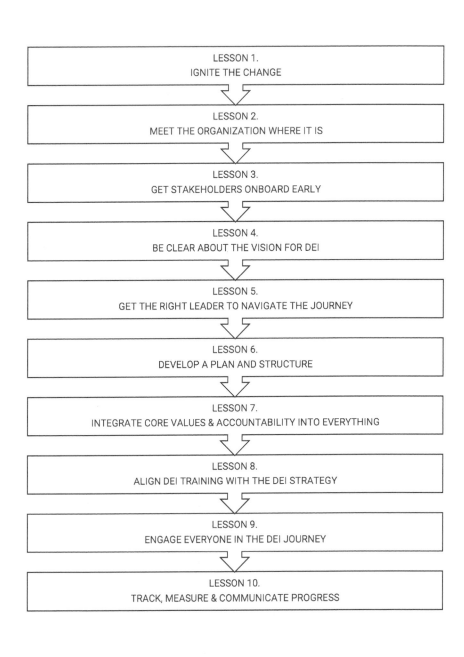

LESSON 1.
IGNITE THE CHANGE

LESSON 2.
MEET THE ORGANIZATION WHERE IT IS

LESSON 3.
GET STAKEHOLDERS ONBOARD EARLY

LESSON 4.
BE CLEAR ABOUT THE VISION FOR DEI

LESSON 5.
GET THE RIGHT LEADER TO NAVIGATE THE JOURNEY

LESSON 6.
DEVELOP A PLAN AND STRUCTURE

LESSON 7.
INTEGRATE CORE VALUES & ACCOUNTABILITY INTO EVERYTHING

LESSON 8.
ALIGN DEI TRAINING WITH THE DEI STRATEGY

LESSON 9.
ENGAGE EVERYONE IN THE DEI JOURNEY

LESSON 10.
TRACK, MEASURE & COMMUNICATE PROGRESS

TABLE OF CONTENTS

FOREWORD I

Nancy M. Schlichting
Retired President and CEO, Henry Ford Health System
2022 Inductee, Healthcare Hall of Fame

I am honored and pleased to write the foreword for Jocelyn Giangrande's book, ***Top-Down Commitment: How Good CEOs Do Diversity and Great Ones Build Culture***. This book is not only practical and relevant, but it is also very timely. I had the privilege of working with Jocelyn for several years at Henry Ford Health System in Detroit. I served in several executive roles at Henry Ford before becoming president and CEO in 2003 (retiring in 2017). It was a tough time in Detroit and at Henry Ford in the early 2000s, but amazing people like Jocelyn gave me confidence and hope that we could turn around Henry Ford and forge a positive path for Detroit under trying economic and social conditions. Despite major population decline (30% over a ten-year period), high poverty and unemployment, the bankruptcies of GM and Chrysler, the City of Detroit becoming the largest municipal bankruptcy in American history, laying off 15% of our workforce in 2002, and low levels of quality, patient and employee satisfaction, in a few years, Henry Ford Health System was able to reach the highest levels of performance on all metrics of our strategic pillars (people, quality and safety, service, growth, academics, community and finance); win the most rigorous and prestigious quality awards (Malcolm Baldrige National Quality Award in 2011 and John Eisenberg Award in 2012); and create high levels of engagement of our employees, physicians and community with a "We're Henry Ford, We Can" culture. The foundation of the culture was the people in our organization and the people we served in the community—embracing the rich diversity of Detroit and the surrounding communities, believing in ourselves, feeling accountable to all of our stakeholders, and integrating diversity into our strategic priorities.

Jocelyn's book is so important as a guide for CEOs to reflect about why and how they are focusing on diversity, equity and inclusion in their companies. It starts by looking inward. What are the values of the CEO and the executive team? What does leadership stand for? How do they behave on a daily basis? How is DEI embedded into everything the organization does? Culture is not something that can be planned and written into a strategic plan. It is created by what happens every day in a company—the decisions that are made, the impact they have on people, the interactions with senior leaders, the tone of communications, the sensitivity to the diversity within the organization and, in the broader community, and most importantly, how people feel. Trust in a company is earned each day and can be destroyed based on one bad decision or insensitive comment.

Jocelyn, and so many other wonderful leaders, have been my teachers throughout my leadership journey. I have made many mistakes, but I have learned from all of them and have changed as a result of them. I was so fortunate to come to Detroit—the best place I have ever lived and worked. The reason that is true is because of the diversity of Detroit, the remarkable people who live and work there, and the grit and resilience of a community that has been through so much. As a gay woman, I, too, have had to endure significant challenges along the way. However, I was accepted in a community that was open to my diversity. I also was honest and open about my mistakes—asking forgiveness and doubling down on my commitment to learn and be responsive to the needs of our community, including our employees and physicians.

Building a culture that authentically embraces diversity, equity and inclusion is not easy. There are many moments of discomfort, failure and disappointment. However, those are also the moments that present the greatest opportunities. Owning the negative experiences that happen in an organization is what creates a culture that respects and includes everyone. Owning them means talking about what happened, how people felt, and what will change.

Perhaps the most significant symbol of our culture at Henry Ford was the strategic framework that guided our work. As CEO, my primary purpose was to create an environment where each person could reach their potential. That meant each employee, each physician, each patient, and each member of the community that interacted with us was able to become the best version of themselves. The strategic framework had seven pillars (people, quality and safety, service, growth, community, academics, and finance). I believed that if we did the first six well, finance would follow, which turned out to be true. We also had a ribbon that was wrapped around the seven pillars—diversity.

Diversity was fully integrated into our strategic work—central to our people strategies by attracting and retaining a diverse workforce leadership team and board of trustees; central to our quality and service strategies by eliminating racial inequities and improving cultural competencies; central to our growth strategies by becoming the preferred healthcare choice by all diverse communities because of our performance; central to our community strategies by becoming a valued partner of local schools, churches and community organizations; central to our academic strategies by educating and training a diverse workforce of the future; and central to our financial strategies by investing in programs that were vital to meeting the needs of the community. The message here is that diversity, equity and inclusion must be both authentically part of the values of leadership and the organization, and fully integrated into the business strategy. I am so grateful that Jocelyn's time at Henry Ford contributed to our progress in the diversity, equity and inclusion journey. Her book promises to advance many companies and organizations forward.

I am confident that CEOs who learn from her experiences and the knowledge she shares in this book will become better leaders, and will build cultures that drive outstanding business results, and enhance people's lives and the world in which we live.

Enjoy!

–Nancy Schlichting

FOREWORD II

Mark Gray
CEO, Katz Media Group

Race, identity, gender, equity and belonging are all deeply emotional topics. To discuss them candidly takes bravery, and Jocelyn empowers CEOs to have those conversations with their teams and employees.

Prioritizing inclusion, equity and diversity in the workplace is not only the right thing to do; it's also plainly good for business. DEI is a vital part of success — and a must for cultivating engaged employees and customers. But how do we go about doing it? I faced this question during the spring of 2020 as an ongoing wave of civil unrest gripped the United States.

As the CEO of Katz Media Group, I lead the largest media representation company in America. Katz provides access to over 250 million active consumers across the country through its three companies — Katz Radio Group, Katz Television Group and Katz Digital Group — serving as the trusted partner to more than 3,300 radio stations, seven hundred television stations, and an expansive portfolio of video and audio digital partners. With offices located in every major city across the country, it is more important now than ever to represent the diverse population that our media partners serve. I tackled this issue head-on as employees reached out to me directly to voice their concerns about where we were as a country and where Katz was specifically addressing diversity, equity and inclusion.

In Katz's long history, we've experienced starts and stops along the way regarding DEI. But the events of that spring ignited a new fervor to put Katz on a fully engaged path, one committed to building a more inclusive and representative workplace where everyone belongs and has the tools and support to thrive and grow. So, we set out to find an expert in the field of DEI to assist us on our journey and I was introduced to Jocelyn. She was recommended for her work with top-ranking leading companies in DEI.

I can recall our first meeting, feeling a bit guarded about sharing Katz's culture with a DEI scholar and expert. But I was immediately put at ease by Jocelyn's calm, confident and inviting nature. That's one of the many great things about Jocelyn: She encourages transparency and openness, simplifying the complex and sometimes intimidating work of DEI in the workplace. She became a true partner, working with us to elevate our company culture.

Over the next few months, I regularly met with Jocelyn to share with her the strides we were making in DEI at Katz Media Group. She shared invaluable input, expertise and guidance on how to strive to be better and do better as a company. Katz has always understood and valued that diversity, equity and inclusion are not only necessary for our employees and workplace culture; it's a common-sense way to help us achieve our business goals. DEI helps attract and retain top talent, make better decisions, meet strategic objectives, obtain market growth, and truly uphold company values.

One of my favorite parts of the book, *Lesson 3: Get Stakeholders Onboard Early*, is a key point I feel is crucial to success. If your leaders aren't willing to walk the walk, why should employees follow? Company standards are set at the top. Getting senior leaders and key stakeholders on board early is critical to ensuring sustainability, commitment and credibility in your organization. Jocelyn helped immensely by holding informative training sessions and workshops with our leadership team to explore DEI in the current climate. She does a fantastic job of explaining DEI in a way that makes the information relevant, understandable and easily digestible. She also implemented a leadership visioning exercise with our executives in which we looked at how DEI can support and drive the mission and vision of our company through our values. Throughout the training, Jocelyn met our leaders where they were and made everyone feel at ease. Her observations of where we are as an organization, and how to keep the momentum going, have been invaluable to me as a CEO.

Jocelyn also helped me be clear about the vision for DEI at Katz. Employees want active communication; they want to know what is being done and be educated on diversity, equity and inclusion. In Part Two of Jocelyn's book, she provides clear guidance on navigating this by setting expectations and being sure to establish a business case rationale that is relevant, meaningful and realistic. She also underscores the importance of establishing an aspirational and clear vision of where you are headed as an organization. With this direction, Katz began an employee resource group called *Stronger Together* to ensure an equal, equitable and inclusive work environment. On a personal level, Jocelyn shared her expertise with me while I prepared for and presented a company town hall held for all Katz employees. It was important for employees to hear from an expert in the field of DEI, and Jocelyn connected so strongly with our team. It's like she was an employee of Katz, talking to them on an equal level. That's how completely emersed in our culture she became.

Overall, Jocelyn's approach to DEI is unique and successful because it's collaborative and thoughtful. She is not prescriptive, offering quick fixes to complex challenges. She makes it clear you will have to put in the hard work, but she's there with you every step of the way in this vital journey. Thankfully for us, Jocelyn poured her best tips into this book, providing a step-by-step guide to replicating this DEI success in your company.

I am honored that Jocelyn asked me to write the foreword for this book and I consider myself truly lucky to have the privilege of learning from Jocelyn and growing as both a human and a CEO. In reading and taking these lessons to heart, you will get so much out of this insightful, eye-opening, easy-to-read book. I encourage you to take the DEI journey with Jocelyn.

Thank you,

-Mark Gray

INTRODUCTION

"Do not strive to be good at doing diversity.
Strive to be great at building a diverse, equitable
and inclusive culture."

Dear CEO,
I am glad you are here. You showed up and that says a lot. So, let us not waste time and cut to the chase. This is your chance to make a difference. Your chance to build the culture you desire and provide what your workforce is seeking. Your chance to ensure your organization is ready for the future. The time is now to get this right and there is a roadmap to do it. However, to make it happen, you must step apart from the good and commit to be part of the great.

Being part of the great may make some of you uncomfortable, mainly because CEOs like you are not seeking greatness for yourself. Instead, you seek greatness for your organization. You are passionate about its sustainability and opportunity to perform at its best. You also want to do right by your people and the communities you serve. Therefore, your goal is to ensure an equal and equitable opportunity for all.

Although the greatness is not about you, it is about your leadership. To build a culture of diversity, equity and inclusion (DEI) takes a great leader. One who understands that DEI is key to organizational greatness. A great leader who is honest about how difficult this work is, yet willing to commit to getting it done. A great leader with top-down commitment.

Top-Down Commitment

Those of you who picked up this book are most likely implementing a DEI strategy. Better yet, you may have already launched one, but you want to ensure you are on the right track. Either way, I am glad you are here. Whether you are launching a strategy or looking to ensure you are on the right course, you are in the right place.

When I originally planned to write this book, I contemplated to whom it should be addressed. However, it did not take long to conclude it had to be you. As CEO, you, and only you, can ensure a DEI culture. Therefore, your top-down commitment is critical.

Top-down commitment does not mean having all of the answers. In fact, great CEOs doing this work seldom know what to do. Instead, they question their perspectives and second guess their approach, knowing they have much to learn. However, it is their humility that leads to greatness. By being humble, they remain open to learning and growing with the organization. That is how they demonstrate top-down commitment.

Over the years, "commitment from the top" has become a cliché regarding DEI. CEOs take pledges and hold up vision statements outlining their commitment. However, their words do not make a difference when their actions say otherwise.

In my opinion, there is a difference between "commitment from the top" and "top-down commitment." "Commitment from the top" focuses on the words. The words of commitment mean more than the role of the top leader. On the other hand, top-down commitment focuses on the role of the leader in DEI.

CEOs who demonstrate top-down commitment understand the difference between saying and doing. They understand that their top-down commitment requires them to act, to build a culture, and to hold everyone accountable. This is what makes a great CEO different from a good one in the name of DEI.

Being part of the great is a big responsibility. It will require work and consistency. You will be put to the test, and you must mean what you say. However, because you are here, I know you are ready for the challenge.

I am also confident you are ready because many of you have contacted me directly via phone calls, video conferences over Zoom, Microsoft Teams, WebEx, and emails to share your vulnerabilities around DEI. I heard your passionate thoughts, concerns, and acknowledgments about your leadership, your organization's DEI efforts, and your introspection about your workplace. You have been transparent. In your own words, you admitted the following:

- *We, as an organization, have not focused on DEI as much as we should.*

- *We put DEI on the back burner, and it has not been a priority.*

- *Our employees are asking us to do more.*

- *I was surprised when I learned how our employees feel when it comes to DEI and how they feel working in our organization.*

- *We held difficult conversations and communications with employees, and it was eye-opening.*

- *I have taken it upon myself to learn more about DEI, racism and inequities.*

- *My children have helped me grow and build awareness and sensitivity.*

- *I now know how much I don't know.*

- *Our employee survey revealed the work we have in front of us.*

- *I am ashamed of our lack of commitment in this area.*
- *We need to weave DEI through the fabric of our organization.*
- *We do not know where to start and when, or if, we are successful.*

Your willingness to engage in uncomfortable conversations about race, inequities and exclusion opened doors for your workforce to provide feedback and share concerns. Feeling the pressure from internal and external communities, over 2,000 of you took a public step. You signed the national *CEO Action for Diversity & Inclusion* pledge, demonstrating your commitment.

The concern you have for your organization, workforce and communities is refreshing. I also appreciate the vulnerability, transparency and the courage to admit you have not done all you can, and should, do in the name of DEI.

It was surprising to hear from you. Usually, when an organization seeks my guidance, my contact is from human resources. However, I am glad it was you. Having the chance to talk with you exclusively about DEI is rare. This book is my chance to take full advantage of the opportunity.

Doing Diversity is Good, But Not Great

You must know by now that this work is not easy. However, it is important, and it cannot be done without you. Yet, most of you are setting yourself up to doing diversity instead of building the culture for DEI to thrive. That is what I hope to prevent with this book.

There is a stark difference between doing diversity and building a DEI culture. Therefore, no matter how much you focus on bringing in diverse talent, conducting DEI trainings, or celebrating diverse communities, it is difficult to obtain a return if you do not have a conducive culture. These efforts are admirable, but they do not get to the core of what makes DEI work. That core is culture.

When it comes to diversity, any company can do it, and many do it well. Most start by launching diversity programs and setting goals, such as more diversity in leadership, on company boards and in their workforce. Some also establish objectives for diverse suppliers, vendors, and multicultural consumers and better ways to serve diverse communities. However, DEI is more than something you do; it is who you are.

DEI is about building an environment that will help you achieve your strategic objectives and enhance your organizational effectiveness. It is also a moral imperative to ensure that you provide an equitable, inclusive opportunity for all communities. Therefore, it is a culture and a way of life. It is embedded in how you operate. That is what makes it more than something you do. However, today, diversity alone is not enough. To excel, grow and sustain requires a culture of diversity, equity and inclusion.

Doing diversity alone is also not great simply because that is what most organizations do. As a consultant, I have worked with over one hundred organizations. Many of them are good at doing diversity. Doing diversity is easy to see, and it is easy to measure. Therefore, it is easy to believe that you have accomplished a goal, made the commitment, and value equity and inclusion.

The truth is most organizations do not have what it takes to make necessary changes to truly benefit from DEI and allow it to thrive. Nor do they trust DEI enough to treat it as a key business strategy. Swamped leaders with competing priorities also hamper efforts.

Building a DEI culture requires organizations to change the status quo. Without a clear business imperative, that change is a hard sell. Although many see its value, few demonstrate that value through actions. Therefore, they often fall back on doing diversity instead. Below are common examples of doing diversity instead of building a culture of DEI:

- Treating the top DEI position like anyone can do it
- Leaders are not held accountable for demonstrating a DEI commitment
- Not being clear about how you define diversity
- Taking a programmatic approach to DEI
- Not giving DEI the power required for change
- Failing to give DEI what it needs to survive
- Not engaging everyone in the organization in the DEI process
- Not spending enough time identifying the right DEI metrics
- Lacking a DEI strategy and rationale that everyone knows and understands
- Not communicating DEI progress and giving up on DEI too soon

There are several other examples beyond this list. If you see any of them playing out in your organization, you may be doing diversity instead of building a DEI culture. However, do not worry. There is hope. The fact that you are here tells me you want to do it right. Together, that is what we will do.

Build It and They Will Come

"Build it and he will come" is a famous quote from the Academy Award-nominated movie *Field of Dreams* starring Kevin Costner. In the 1989 film, Costner plays a farmer who builds a baseball field in his cornfield that attracts the ghosts of baseball legends. Costner's character hears a voice telling him to follow his dream—to build the ideal baseball field and he will come. He does, and his dream comes true.

There is another quote in the movie that does not get as much attention. That is, *"They're all welcome here."* Costner's character not only builds it, but he also ensures that all the legends feel welcomed.

Although I do not believe in ghosts, I believe in the concept. If you build the right culture and ensure that all are welcomed, diversity will come. Focus on the culture and it will not only come, but it will thrive. You will see your organizational dreams come true.

In the book, *The Person You Mean to Be: How Good People Fight Bias* by Dolly Chugh, the author points out that there are either believers or builders when it comes to bias. Chugh states that believers believe that "Bias in all forms is wrong." Builders, on the other hand, as described by Chugh, work on building the skills to act on their beliefs. Builders move to make things better, to make a difference. I see that same analogy for DEI. When it comes to DEI, there are DEI believers and there are DEI builders.

DEI believers do diversity by stating what they believe. However, DEI builders take action to build the cultures they believe in. Building requires you to get your hands dirty. Building requires you to make tough decisions and to put your words into action. Builders ensure accountability and are selective about who they let into their cultures and who gets to stay.

Builders also do not worry about perfection; they are not afraid of scrutiny. Believers, on the other hand, worry about looking good and avoiding scrutiny. They often window dress with lofty statements, diverse-looking websites and publications. Builders are comfortable with the uncomfortable as they build and see the long-term gain of a DEI culture. Believers, on the other hand, are for immediate gratification.

This Book is for DEI Builders

This book is for the DEI builders. As a DEI builder, you build cultures, brick by brick. You will get dirty. You will make mistakes. You will have doubts. However, that is part of the journey. You do not have to be perfect to be successful. You just need to commit to staying a builder. With that mindset, you can do it.

As I stated before, this work is not easy. However, rest assured with peace of mind because I am here to help. Together, we will tap into my expertise as a consultant and practitioner, as well as my personal experience. Working in diverse industries such as human services, higher education, hospitality and health care provided extensive experience in the dynamics of building DEI cultures and the impact on organizational performance.

As a human services worker, working in diverse communities not only helped reveal the different challenges communities face, but it also helped me understand how to bring diverse, innovative solutions. I learned how different people require different solutions. You must meet communities where they are.

In higher education, working in diversity recruitment and advising, I used cross-cultural communication to educate, connect and engage with potential students, parents and educational professionals from various backgrounds. The ability to flex my style and approach to build bridges of trust was a huge lesson. It also taught me how to build relationships with diverse groups and the importance of listening to understand. I was able to seek ways to remove barriers to ensure equity and inclusion.

As an executive in hospitality for the *#1 Company for Diversity on the 2021 DiversityInc's Top 50 Companies for Diversity*, I provided experience in connecting a DEI culture to organizational performance. Leading workforce strategies, human resources and DEI initiatives, the use of metrics, data and assessments were paramount. I learned to make the connection between diverse, engaged and trained employees and bottom-line outcomes. Communication was vital to driving performance.

Serving as an executive leading talent selection, workforce compliance and DEI initiatives in healthcare for an organization ranking number two on the 2020 *Forbes Best Companies for Diversity* and two years as #1 on *DiversityInc's Best in Healthcare for Diversity*, I gained experience building DEI cultures in a complex, fast-paced industry. This helped hone skills, connecting DEI to business operations. I also gained extensive experience in integrating DEI into policy, practice, programs and procedures, ensuring compliant, equitable environments.

During my career, I also worked on and led intercompany diversity boards, committees and councils with members representing various industries. Designing over two hundred and fifty DEI trainings, thousands of leaders have attended my workshops and seminars. My certification as a Cornell University Certified Diversity Professional (CCDP), as well as my degree in psychology with a specialization in human behavior and organizational dynamics, equips me to take a strategic approach and opened doors to teach courses at universities and colleges.

As an independent consultant for nearly fifteen years, I partnered with over one hundred organizations, providing consultation and expertise on building inclusive cultures, positioning DEI as a business strategy and inclusive leadership.

My experience as an African American woman is also valuable. My race and gender have often resulted in being "the diverse student," "the diverse candidate," "the diverse hire," "the diverse leader," "the diverse board member," and "the diverse vendor." Therefore, I have experienced being that person who helps institutions and organizations check the box, simply meeting diversity goals and/ or mandates.

This experience is beneficial to my work in DEI. I know what it feels like to have to fit in and prove you are more than a "diversity person." I also know what it feels like to be embraced, respected, and valued as an outsider. Therefore, my professional experience, education and passion provided a unique observation of organizational dynamics, cultures, and what it takes to embrace DEI. Therefore, I bring this experience to you.

As you read this book, know that I earned a reputation for having the courage to ask the right questions and challenge leaders. I plan to live up to that reputation with you. My goal is to provide a strategic approach to DEI and prevent the temptation of just being good by "doing" diversity and checking the box.

Building a DEI culture is a journey, and this book will guide you on the journey. As we work together, I will not bombard you with statistics about why DEI is good for business. You already know that. Instead, I will be straight about what it takes to build a DEI culture, what could hold you back, and how to set yourself and your organization up for success. I will also not sugarcoat anything. I will share the good, the bad, and the ugly.

Having viewed many organizations from the outside, I see the roadblocks, the saboteurs, and the barriers to moving the needle. Yet, I learned many lessons while guiding organizations on the DEI journey. We will leverage my lessons learned to guide your journey.

As with most journeys, you get better results, have a better experience, and have a better outcome if you prepare for the trip. This book is not only designed to help you prepare. It will also help plan the direction, create a roadmap, and outline adequate resources to get there.

Our DEI Culture Journey

Our DEI culture journey is divided into the following four parts, answering key journey questions:

PART ONE:
Preparing for the DEI Journey
What to Do First?

PART TWO:
Setting the Journey Direction
Where Are You Going?

PART THREE:
Outlining the Journey Roadmap
How Do You Get There?

PART FOUR:
Establishing Journey Checkpoints
Are You Moving in the Right Direction?

To get the most out of our journey, go through each of the four parts in sequential order. This will ensure you build the proper foundation and include best practices for a DEI culture. However, you do not have to incorporate all the lessons to be great. No one shoe fits all. This is strictly a guide to help set you up for success, sustainability, and credibility—all of which are important for this work.

I look forward to going on this journey with you. Together, let us not do diversity. Instead, let us start building a culture of DEI. It is the great thing to do.

Here we go!

This is your chance to...

Make a difference

Build the culture you desire

Provide what your workforce is seeking

Ensure your organization is positioned for the future

Be great for the excellence of your organization

**"You do not have to be perfect to get DEI right.
You just have to stay committed from the top-down."**

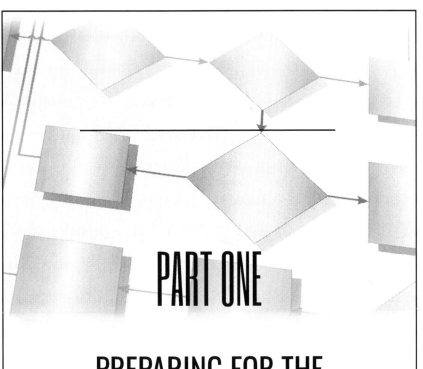

PART ONE

PREPARING FOR THE DEI CULTURE JOURNEY

What to Do First?

Establish the Right DEI Mindset

To make the transition from doing diversity to building a DEI culture, you must get into the DEI cultural mindset.

Remember that you are a DEI builder. As a DEI builder, you build culture, brick by brick. You will get dirty. You will make mistakes. You will have doubts. However, this is part of the journey. You do not have to be perfect to be successful. You simply need to commit to staying a builder. With that mindset, you can do it.

The DEI cultural mindset is focused on the following Five Key Steps:

The Five Key Steps to a DEI Cultural Mindset:

1. Change your view of DEI.
2. Realize it is a journey, not a destination.
3. Understand the challenges of building a DEI culture.

4. Avoid common DEI pitfalls.

5. Transform to an open and transparent organization.

Step 1. Change Your View of DEI

The first step to adopting the DEI cultural mindset is to stop looking at DEI as something you do. Instead, look at it as building a high-performing organization. With that mindset, it becomes who you are as an organization, not something you do today and forget tomorrow. It is through DEI that you attract and retain the best talent, build an environment where everyone excels, and create processes that enhance organizational effectiveness. You must make it part of the business.

As a DEI consultant, I struggle with the concept of DEI. It makes it appear as if it is an addition to the business instead of the best way to do business. When we put a label on it, we put it in a box. Soon, DEI becomes this mysterious thing that we have to understand and do. The DEI cultural mindset takes it out of the box and integrates it into the business. Stop thinking of doing DEI. Move to thinking of how to enhance your organization through it.

Step 2. Realize It Is a Journey, not a Destination

Often, I use the metaphor of going on a diet versus adopting a healthy lifestyle when explaining the difference between the DEI journey and the DEI destination mindset. For example, when one goes on a diet, they often pick a destination goal of how much weight they wish to lose. They spend days weighing themselves and watching the pounds drop with elation. If they reach their destination, they feel accomplished.

Weight loss is an outstanding achievement. However, often as I have seen with friends and relatives who diet, it is not easy to sustain. Most people regain the weight. On the other hand, those who adopt a healthy lifestyle and integrate systemic behavioral changes have a better chance of sustaining weight loss.

Making a lifestyle change is difficult because it requires a long-term commitment that is not always easy or pleasant to sustain. This commitment is what deters many and leads to taking the diet route instead. The same is true when it comes to taking the DEI journey. Understanding the difference between a journey and a destination is critical to adopting the DEI culture mindset.

According to Merriam-Webster, a **journey** is defined as, *"an act or instance of traveling from one place to another."*

Realizing that building a DEI culture is a journey makes it clear that when you embark on the journey, you are moving from one cultural place to another. This will require you to take certain systemic steps to get to the other place. Adopting a DEI culture mindset acknowledges that you cannot make the passage unless you take those steps. Therefore, obtaining a DEI culture is not guaranteed without doing the work. That is what makes it a journey.

On the other hand, Merriam-Webster defines a **destination** as, *"the purpose for which something is predetermined."*

Therefore, when you view DEI as a destination, as many organizations do, you set yourself up for the belief that your arrival to a DEI culture is guaranteed. With that mindset, you will likely claim your destination before you arrive. Organizations who view DEI as a destination focus on the end point, without considering the systemic steps required to get there.

Eventually, the destination is glorified, prompting a mirage of fancy diversity celebrations, the quest for diverse faces, and DEI lofty commitment statements. This mirage creates false perceptions that the destination is near or that you have arrived. However, these efforts will not get you from your current cultural place to a DEI culture. It will only create a destination oasis you may never reach or sustain.

Step 3. Understand the Challenges of Building a DEI Culture

Building a DEI culture is not easy. There are many challenges and obstacles along the way. These challenges cause organizations to fall into the trap of doing diversity instead. Let us look at some of these challenges.

CHALLENGE #1
The Change Intolerance

Most organizations, like most people, hate change. Change is scary and many avoid it. Therefore, it is common for an organization, whether consciously or unconsciously, to be change intolerant. However, a DEI culture often requires a lot of changes, such as:

- Changes in how leaders lead
- Changes in how employees interact
- Changes in how policies and procedures are applied
- Changes in the communities you serve and products and services you produce
- Changes in how you measure progress, performance and outcomes
- Changes in how you communicate and who gets a voice
- Changes in how you select, promote and develop talent
- Changes in how you make decisions
- Changes in how you operate

These changes disrupt the comfort of many organizational leaders and those who enjoy the status quo.

Lastly, change is also frightening. It is scary to change things when you do not know how those changes will impact you and the organization. When the future is unknown, it may cause anxiety and create uncertainty about who will fit into the change. It is easier to continue doing what you know than to do something new. It is also challenging to determine how much change is needed and how far down the change must occur. However, no matter what, DEI requires change and that takes tolerance.

CHALLENGE #2
The Big Job

"This is a big job!" were the first words describing a Chief Diversity Officer (CDO) position for the vacation rental company Airbnb. To keep up on how organizations see this role, I often review job descriptions for CDOs. I must admit I have not been impressed. It is rare to run across an organization that gets that this is a big job! Over the years, not much has changed in terms of the role and responsibility. Although the terminology has changed, using buzzwords like equity, belonging, culture, etc., the responsibilities still focus on doing diversity, bringing in the numbers, and making the organization look good as a committed corporate citizen.

Most also still link the job with human resources or other responsibilities and keep it below the senior executive level. However, when I saw the words, "This is a big job!" on my computer screen, I saw words of courage, commitment and truth.

What makes this job big is that culture is delicate and hard to transform. Whenever you have more than one person in the room, you increase the potential of conflict, misunderstandings, and exclusion. That alone makes diversity and inclusion challenging.
If you bring in equity, that is another component to manage and sustain, often causing changes in how organizations operate, behave and lead. People are complex and the more diversity, the more complexity. Therefore, to believe that one can hang out a diversity, equity and inclusion sign, launch trainings and promote a diversity mission, vision and value statement, and say you have DEI, is unrealistic. To do it right requires a new way of thinking and focus. That is a big job!

7

CHALLENGE #3
The Equity and Inclusion Delusion

Many companies suffer from what I call the equity and inclusion delusion. The fact is most company cultures are exclusive. This exclusion happens in many ways, and, in most cases, it is not intentional. Informal networks, access to information, lack of oversight and outdated practices cause organizations to unintentionally exclude.

To succeed and advance, you must know the unwritten rules, influencers, advancement paths, opportunities, mentors and sponsors. This information is available to those in certain positions or with connections. Others lacking this knowledge, or the connections, are excluded.

Ensuring equity and inclusion requires measuring and tracking the impact of policies, practices, and procedures on the workforce. You must also look for trends and patterns that promote or prevent segments of the organization from advancing, developing, or contributing.

Transitioning from doing diversity to building a culture that embraces it is difficult. The intolerance for change, the fact that it is a big job, as well as having to dig deep to see where your exclusion resides is challenging. It is also difficult to sustain the culture of DEI.

Unless you take a systemic and integrated approach, it is easy to fall into the trap of doing diversity, even if it is the wrong thing to do.

Step 4. Avoid Common DEI Pitfalls

There are many pitfalls that organizations fall into on the DEI journey. However, there are three major pitfalls that lead to "doing" diversity instead of building a DEI culture.

Below are common pitfalls and the disservice they cause:

1. Making it about certain groups. You cannot be inclusive by being exclusive. Leaving segments of your workforce out of diversity is not the best way to drive a DEI culture. When it comes to a high-performing organization, it requires all perspectives, ideas and engagement. Therefore, you must include everyone, including white males, in the equation. Everyone must be part of the solution for a DEI culture.

2. Measuring success on what you see instead of organizational impact. Representation in numbers, accolades and awards, and dollars spent are visible and easy to measure. Therefore, they are the go-to metrics to determine success. However, it is employee morale, having all voices heard, total engagement, removing barriers to ensure a level playing field, and treating people with respect and dignity that are the true measures of a DEI culture. When you have that, you get the return on efforts.

3. Failing to prepare your organization for the culture shift. If you do not assess where your organization is on the DEI culture scale and prepare it for where it is going, you do a disservice to your people, leaders, and workplace. You must do the work to get ready for the journey. This may require cultural assessments, training, education, and changing policies, procedures, and practices. Put in the work up front, or you will just scratch the surface. You won't make the necessary systemic changes to benefit from a DEI culture.

Step 5. Transform to an Open and Transparent Organization

"A transparent organization focuses on three important words: communication, honesty, and trust."

Transparency: "The quality that makes it possible to see through something." - Merriam Webster

One of the big cultural shifts for an organization is understanding that a DEI culture is a transparent and open culture. In a DEI culture, trust is often built through the exchange of open and honest information. Therefore, communication is key.

Creating various avenues to share and exchange information frequently and in many formats, is required. According to a 2022 *Fast Company* article, **Leaders: This is What More Communication Should Look Like**, 90% of surveyed employees want leaders to communicate at least once per week. Therefore, organizations must make the paradigm shift from selective communication to over-communication.

Keeping people informed of changes, decisions, accomplishments, and failures is a critical feature in a DEI culture. Bringing your communities along as you move through the DEI journey and all other transformations, acquisitions and shifts are essential. Nothing breaks trust more than the failure to inform constituents and keeping them out of the loop.

When it comes to DEI, your communities need to know what DEI means to you as an organization, why are you committed to it, and how it will impact them. They also need to know about opportunities, and receive open and honest feedback on performance, the status of goals and objectives, as well as expectations. This requires two-way feedback channels to share information, ideas, solutions and opinions to the organization and its leaders. Transparency also includes having opportunities to ask questions and seek information.

Adopting the DEI cultural mindset is an important preparatory step on the DEI journey. You must understand that DEI is not a destination; it is an ongoing journey. It requires change and everyone will be anxious about the change. Therefore, you must enhance your tolerance by taking the steps to prepare all stakeholders to embrace and support the changes.

Building a DEI culture is indeed a big job. However, you know that it is key to your organization's future. If you incorporate best practices, avoid the common pitfalls, and build trust through transparency, you can build and sustain a fruitful, authentic DEI culture.

Now let us embark on the DEI journey!

LESSON 1
Ignite the Change

As CEO, you must demonstrate that the DEI culture journey has begun, and the commitment is here to stay.

"It is easy to tell if an organization stands a chance of sustaining the DEI journey by observing the CEO."

Top-Down Commitment

As CEO, you have the power to change the culture. You probably knew that already. The same is true when it comes to DEI. Contrary to what you may believe, you have the capacity to change to a DEI culture much quicker than you may expect. Let me share a cultural shift story to demonstrate what I mean.

I once worked for a company that hired a new CEO from another industry. His marching orders were to whip the company into shape. From the first day of his tenure, you felt a cultural shift. He made it clear that he was not there to make friends and stated with conviction that he expected results. His behavior in executive meetings was consistent, conveying that he only wanted to hear results with no "excuses."

Within months, it was a different company. New hires who reflected cutthroat values were brought in, and leaders stopped collaborating as they had in the past and instead became siloed, refusing to share information. Soon, employees who were a fit for the previous culture found themselves unfit for the new one and left. He created a new toxic culture.

This story highlights how a CEO used his power to change culture quickly. Although he did many of the wrong things for the health of the company, there are transferable takeaways to changing to a DEI culture.

Those takeaways are:

- Leading with conviction
- Communicating expectations clearly and consistently
- Demonstrating commitment through attitudes, behaviors, and beliefs

If a CEO uses his or her power for the good of DEI, leads with conviction, communicates expectations often, and demonstrates the culture shift consistently in behaviors, attitudes, and beliefs, it will expedite cultural change. Therefore, you must mean what you say and prove it through your actions every day. That is what it means to have top-down commitment.

When it comes to building a DEI culture, your role is critical. Every comment you make, every action you take, and the behavior you accept will be tested through the DEI lens. Everyone is watching you. They are looking to determine if the DEI commitment is real, and your actions tell them a lot. I know because your employees tell me what they see and whether they believe you. Honestly, most do not find you credible regarding the DEI culture shift.

When it comes to credibility, many of you are doing a poor job. Your lack of action, lack of consistency, and inability to hold others accountable leads to mistrust. You must demonstrate your commitment daily and reinforce it in the minds of those you lead. Your workforce is savvy, and they know insincerity when they see it.

This responsibility often requires a notable change on behalf of a CEO. The journey will get off to a rough start without it. So let us discuss this change for you.

Be Open to Change You!

Change is difficult. Period. In most organizations, change is an unfriendly word. It is often the biggest barrier to building a DEI culture. However, if you cannot embrace change, you will find this journey impossible. The most notable change I see for CEOs like yourself is changing how they look at things. Building, leading, and sustaining a DEI culture will require you to:

- Change the way you look at your organization.
- Change the way you look at your leadership.
- Change the way you look at your direct reports and leadership team.
- Change the way you look at your workforce.
- Change the way you look at your communities.
- Change the way you look at DEI.

I advise every CEO to start with a new lens. As you look through the new lens, know that I was not the one to coin the phrase, "... change the way you look at things." It was motivational, and *New York Times* bestselling author Wayne Dyer said, *"If you change the way you look at things, the things you look at change."*

DEI requires you to look at things through a different lens. When you do that, the things you look at do indeed change. You begin to look at things from many perspectives. You become open and appreciate various opinions. Eventually, you will find that your understanding, awareness, and sensitivity expand, and you can put yourself in someone else's shoes.

Our teams, our workforces, and our communities expect leaders, like yourself, to change the way you look at things, hoping that the things you look at change. Before we explore the changes required of you, I encourage you to obtain guidance and support.

Consider Inclusive Coaching

In my experience, few CEOs seek coaching to enhance or develop inclusive leadership skills. However, it is highly recommended. Leading a DEI organization and making the transformation is difficult. It's even more difficult with all the competing challenges and priorities CEOs face.

Also, as humans, we fall into comfort zones and habits. We surround ourselves with like-minded individuals. So even if you have diversity around you, your actions often indirectly create homogeneous cultures.

No matter how strong your commitments are, your daily actions make the difference. People often follow your lead, especially direct reports. They get in line, tell you what you want to hear, and eventually learn the norms of expected behavior. Therefore, it is critical to obtain objective guidance to help you see this dynamic and how to work around it.

Having a confidant in the form of an inclusive coach is important on the DEI journey. I have coached senior leaders to guide them in demonstrating DEI commitments while leveraging and developing their inclusive leadership skills. A good inclusive leadership coach can help you leverage your strengths and be objective about your blind spots and areas for enhanced awareness. They should also help you sort through your DEI questions and opportunities.

Coaching may also provide tools, approaches, and skill-building to strengthen your communication, listening, and observation skills to support a DEI culture. If DEI is new to you, or if you believe you would benefit from guidance in this area, consider obtaining an inclusive coach. You do not have to do it alone.

Changing Your Lens

Changing your lens will help expedite your transformation into a more inclusive, equitable leader. Let us review some of these new ways of looking at things.

Change the Way You Look at Your Organization

Use the new lens to identify organizational areas that support DEI and ways they may be replicated and leveraged. Also, seek to find the pockets of resistance and how they may be brought along on the journey. Finally, use your new lens to find answers to whether your systems are set up to support DEI and see if your internal culture matches the external image.

Change the Way You Look at Your Own Leadership

Use the new lens to look in the mirror at your leadership style and approach. Look to see if you consistently demonstrate DEI through your actions. Through the lens, determine if your behavior and focus say DEI is a priority. Does the lens see how you are willing to make changes, difficult decisions, investments, and sacrifices to make DEI work? Lastly, does the lens reveal how you model the importance of DEI training, education, and development to the DEI journey?

Change the Way You Look at Your Leadership Teams

Use the lens to determine if your leadership team is as diverse as you need it to be. Are all diverse perspectives heard, leveraged, and rewarded? Do they have the skills to be inclusive leaders, and do they live your values consistently through their behaviors? Seek to find those leaders who actively support DEI and determine how they may coach others along the way. Also, look through the lens to seek leaders who do not actively support DEI and sabotage efforts. This observation could reveal which ones honestly need to be terminated.

Look through the lens daily to see with whom you connect more than others, who you sponsor, mentor, and support. Look to see who has access to you, which voices are heard the most, and which voices are silent.

Change the Way You Look at Your Workforce

Use the lens to see your workforce clearly and objectively. Do you see engaged, respected, and valued employees at all levels? How much do you know them, their needs, their challenges, their ambitions? Can you see their pain points? What are their behaviors and feedback telling you? Is it clear where DEI is working for them and where it is not?

Change the Way You Look at Your Communities

Use the lens to look at the communities you serve. Do you see how you are meeting their needs and the opportunities to do better? Does the lens show any discrepancies in how you serve the external community versus the internal community? Is it clear which communities need to be considered today and for tomorrow? How can communities become assets to you on the DEI journey?

Change the Way You Look at DEI

Use the lens to look at things from the mindset of how "we can" instead of why "we cannot." For example, does the lens see DEI as disruptive, complicated, or a burden? Are you constantly worrying about offending others and saying or doing the wrong thing? Or does your lens see DEI as an opportunity to build a culture where all may thrive and improve organizational effectiveness?

Lastly, use the lens to see opportunities and identify tangible ways you can actively demonstrate that the DEI culture change has begun and is here to stay.

CHAPTER SUMMARY
Lesson 1: Ignite the Change

"As CEO, you must demonstrate that the DEI culture journey has begun, and the commitment is here to stay."

KEY LESSONS

1. When it comes to the success of DEI, the commitment must come from the top down.

2. You have the capacity to expedite the change by leading with conviction, communicating expectations often, and demonstrating commitment through your actions.

3. Inclusive coaching is a great way to build skills, engage a confidant and obtain objective guidance on the DEI journey.

4. Change the way you look at things to see if the things you look at change.

5. Remember, everyone is watching you to see if DEI is here to stay.

LESSON 2
Meet the Organization Where it Is

Don't assume the organization is ready to embrace DEI. Instead, meet the current culture where it is and prepare it for the journey.

"I never met a CEO who has not asked, "What's the biggest mistake when launching a DEI journey?" My answer is always the same, failure to assess if the organization is ready."

How Ready is The Organization?

Ask yourself: Is the current culture ready to embrace a DEI culture or will it be eaten for lunch (meaning the strategy will not survive the culture)? Every organization must answer this question.

Assessing readiness is an important step in determining what organizational strengths will help your DEI efforts and what threats may hamper them.

Organizational strengths that may help your DEI efforts may include:

- Universal understanding of the DEI business imperative
- Trust and understanding of differences
- Inclusive and equitable policies and practices
- Open and frequent communication
- Quest for continuous improvement

Organizational threats that could hamper DEI efforts may include:

- Pockets of resistance and individuals willing to sabotage efforts
- DEI rumors and misinterpretations
- Exclusive behaviors and previous DEI failed attempts
- Mistrust, divisions, and tolerance of exclusive behaviors
- Lack of communication and misunderstandings

In my experience, most organizations require some form of preparation to embrace a DEI culture. This preparation may include communications to build understanding, training on basic DEI skills, or simply answering frequent DEI questions. This preparation should be done before you launch a DEI strategy. A readiness assessment is a good first step.

A readiness assessment helps reveal the gaps between your current cultural state and where you are today compared to where you want to go. This also helps determine the necessary preparation before you launch.

There are many ways to determine readiness. For example, some organizations conduct cultural audits or assessments, employee focus groups, or employee surveys. The goal is to determine the level of the organization's readiness so you may meet the organization where it is.

READINESS STEP 1:
Determine Your Current Level of DEI Readiness

There are various stages of readiness when it comes to an organization's ability to embrace a DEI culture. Cornell University ILR School, Management Programs readiness model, the model I often use with clients, outlines four (stages of readiness). They are as follows in ascending order:

Stage 1.   *Intolerant or Homogeneous*

Stage 2.   *Tolerant or Compliant*

Stage 3.   *Acceptance*

Stage 4.   *Fully Integrated or Fully Inclusive*

Below are descriptions of each culture and level of organizational readiness:

1. Intolerant or Homogeneous Cultures

This organizational culture is *"homogeneous and intolerant of differences, often viewing any changes as disruptive and threatening."*

In my experience, an intolerant culture is most resistant to change. DEI is seen as a threat. These types of cultures often have a dominant group who holds the power, makes the decisions, and hires those who "fit." Ultimately, this practice results in a workforce or leadership where everyone has the same attitudes, behaviors, and beliefs.

If you find yourself here, preparing your culture, especially your leaders, is highly recommended through extensive communications, awareness, and sensitivity training. Care is required to help the dominant group understand why the change is needed, how it will benefit the organization and its impact on them.

Failure to prepare this culture can be detrimental to progress and the embrace of DEI required for success.

2. Tolerant Cultures:

This organizational culture is *"tolerant of differences, but only focuses on diversity to stay out of trouble."*

In my experience, this is a "check-the-box" culture. They often focus on external recognition, such as winning DEI awards, writing lofty statements, and holding DEI celebrations and programs. When it comes to diversity in representation, some feel standards are lowered to accommodate specific groups.

Many see DEI programs as a way to avoid liability. Diversity is often prevalent at lower levels in the organization yet limited in leadership. A lack of trust is common in these cultures.

If you find yourself here, it is recommended to prepare by building trust in the DEI commitment. Senior leaders must demonstrate commitment through communications. Actions such as partaking in trainings, implementing accountability, and addressing exclusive practices show a strategic and systemic approach. If you have had false starts in the past, acknowledge the history, and communicate how this time is different.

3. Acceptance Cultures:

This type of organizational culture is *"an organization that accepts diversity and understands the business case for DEI. In addition, commitment is often demonstrated through actions such as inclusive policies and practices."*

In my experience, this type of culture, having launched its DEI culture journey, is in the beginning stages of a strategic, integrated approach. Efforts to date build trust that the organization is committed and moving in the right direction. These types of cultures have consistency between the internal and external faces of the organization when it comes to DEI.

If you find yourself here, you are in good shape. You have a foundation of trust to continue the DEI journey. Recommended preparation should include effective communication about where you are on the journey and where you are going next. It is important to maintain trust. So, be honest about progress and setbacks. Include employees in the solution and let them know how they may engage in the process.

4. Fully Integrated Cultures:

This type of organizational culture is an *"inclusive organizational culture where DEI is fully integrated into the fabric of the organization."*

In my experience, organizations achieving and sustaining this type of culture is rare, but possible. In fully integrated cultures, diverse perspectives, opinions, and experiences are sought and fully utilized. This culture sees open communication and transparency as the key to success and organizational effectiveness. However, they are not perfect. Perfection is not the key; continuous improvement is.

They also have many other positive attributes, such as:

- Robust DEI metrics are aligned with bottom-line outcomes.
- Continuous improvement is valued, and training and education are important to treating members with respect.
- Performance is measured on behaviors and core values.
- Employees have a voice, opportunities to contribute, and talent is developed and leveraged.

If you find yourself here, move forward. You are fully prepped.

PREPARING THE ORGANIZATION FOR A DEI CULTURE

Organizational readiness may be conducted by using an experienced facilitator to survey selected leaders. Asking leaders to share concrete examples of behaviors exhibited in your organization is an organic way to determine readiness. This may also be conducted with selected DEI council or committee members. You must trust leaders or members to keep information confidential and have a legal review of the process.

Below is what I advise clients to do to prepare for building a DEI culture based on the types of culture they have currently:

- Build awareness by helping leaders and the workforce understand why you are launching this journey and the business imperative DEI.

- Outline the risks to the organization if you do not take the DEI journey and what you hope to gain.

- Explain why the current state needs to change and connect the change to the success of the organization in the future.

- Build credibility by utilizing top senior leaders to communicate messages and build awareness.

- Answer how the change may impact those involved, including leaders and communities internal and external to the organization.

- Conduct basic awareness and sensitivity training to help leaders understand the fundamentals of a DEI culture and the best practices of DEI as a business strategy.

- Identify pockets of resistance and provide more robust preparation, communication and awareness. Outline behavioral expectations.

- Dispel DEI rumors and potential misunderstandings and misinterpretations.

Although completing this exercise may delay your launch, skipping this will be a disservice to teams and hamper efforts. Therefore, meet the organization where it is. Get it what it needs to adequately prepare. It will set you up for long-term success.

CHAPTER SUMMARY
Lesson 2: Meet the Organization Where It Is

Don't assume the organization is ready to embrace a DEI culture. Instead, meet the current culture where it is and prepare it for the journey.

KEY LESSONS

1. Examine your organizational strengths and threats that could promote DEI and potentially hamper it.

2. Access your cultural readiness by assessing where your current culture fits on the stages to a fully integrated culture.

3. Meet your organization where it is and do adequate preparation through communications, training and education, and awareness building.

4. Consider bringing in a professional consultant or facilitator to lead focus groups or to administer assessments and surveys.

5. Review any legal ramifications in your assessments, surveys and responses.

Get Stakeholders on Board Early

Getting senior leaders and key stakeholders on board early is critical to ensuring sustainability, commitment, and credibility.

"Your leadership must be invested in the DEI journey from the onset, or you will have an uphill battle."

Are your senior leaders and key stakeholders willing to be ambassadors and promoters for DEI? This is an important question to consider. When it comes to building a DEI culture, leaders play a major role and must be willing to:

- Change their leadership behaviors
- Embrace training and education for themselves and direct reports
- Hold themselves and others accountable to a DEI culture
- Communicate DEI progress and setbacks
- Remain open, honest, and transparent

It is easy to believe your senior leaders and key stakeholders have bought into the DEI journey. However, you must take time to confirm if it is true. They must be ready to embrace systemic change and help lead it.

Many senior leadership teams are ready to "do" diversity. However, few have bought into building a systemic DEI culture. Most are expecting to do diversity by:

- Hiring more diverse team members
- Attending DEI training
- Participating in DEI celebrations and discussions
- Being subjected to some sort of assessment or survey

To them, DEI is the right thing to do. But, often, they underestimate the impact on themselves, the role they will play, and how the DEI journey is aligned with their strategic objectives.

Having senior leadership and key stakeholder buy-in is critical. However, buy-in does not mean they understand the importance of it. Most leaders know that. Instead, are they able to articulate why it is important? This articulation must clarify the business rationale for your company, industry, and future growth. And, most importantly, their belief that it is key to your organization's sustainability and effectiveness.

If your senior leaders are incapable of leading the journey, you may find yourself "doing" diversity instead of building a DEI culture. The best way to get them on board is to get them involved early in the process. Before you launch, they must be invested in the business case, initial visioning, and an assessment.

Senior leaders play a key role in your culture today and where you are going tomorrow. The workforce looks to leadership to determine DEI's credibility. They also look to them for answers to DEI questions and concerns. Finally, they look to leadership to understand DEI's impact on them. Therefore, senior leadership must be committed themselves to the DEI journey.

Steps to Leadership Buy-In

"To get the buy-in of your leadership, don't tell them why DEI is a business imperative; instead, have them tell you."

The best way to get your leadership on board is to engage them in the DEI visioning. This is best accomplished with senior leaders, not operational or front-line ones. Senior leaders are the decision-makers. They have the authority to make change and understand your business for today and in the future. Therefore, they are better suited to understand how DEI is important to organizational effectiveness.

Most leaders do not get on board unless they can see a clear line of sight to DEI's positive impact on the business. Therefore, take them through an analysis to determine if, how, and why DEI is important to your organization's future.

Step 1. What is the track record?

The first step to getting your leaders on board, and articulating the vision, is to have them hold up a mirror to your organization's commitment to DEI. This review will provide a clear picture of your track record.

- Have you had failed attempts?
- Have you developed a reputation for living up to your commitment?
- Is this the first public commitment?

To determine where you are going in the future, it is essential to know where you have been. You must acknowledge your history before you move forward for the following reasons:

- To avoid repeating mishaps and mistakes
- To address any challenges that have consistently surfaced in previous efforts

- To evaluate if past commitments have failed and created mistrust
- To be honest with yourself about your past performance

Step 2. What are the DEI wins, and where are the opportunities?

Another important exercise is identifying your current and past DEI wins and opportunities for change. This information is essential for developing the business case and information that may be used for the strategic planning and focused goals and objectives.

Some questions to explore:

1. What success have we had around DEI?
2. What is welcoming and working well?
3. What DEI efforts have been endorsed, embraced, or appreciated?
4. What positive feedback have we received around DEI initiatives?
5. What is not working or not welcoming around DEI?
6. What negative feedback have we received around DEI?

Step 3. What is the business rationale for focusing on a DEI culture?

Having your senior leaders determine the business rationale for DEI is extremely important to buy-in. This step takes it from just the "right thing to do" to becoming a key business strategy. When they see the alignment between DEI and meeting strategic objectives, they often get on board. This also helps see the role they play and why it is important.

Questions to consider are:

- Why do we need to focus on DEI?
- What will happen if we do not focus on DEI?
- What do we have to gain from DEI?

When your senior leaders and key stakeholders are on board, your workforce will see the credibility of your DEI efforts. Therefore, engaging them in the beginning, is beneficial. They play a key role in your culture. Your journey's success depends on whether they embrace it and step into their respective roles. They will only do that when they have truly bought into the journey. Then, they can be ambassadors of DEI and help you lead it.

CHAPTER SUMMARY
Lesson 3: Get Stakeholders on Board Early

"Getting senior leaders and key stakeholders on board early is critical to ensuring sustainability, commitment, and credibility."

KEY LESSONS

1. Determine if your senior leaders and key stakeholders are truly on board and bought into a DEI culture.

2. Help clarify the difference between "doing" diversity versus making systemic change and sharing how a DEI culture will impact them as leaders.

3. Consider using an experienced facilitator to engage leadership in the DEI visioning and determining the business rationale for a DEI culture.

4. Equip them with training, education, and resources to assist in articulating the DEI vision and to demonstrate DEI behaviors.

5. Use the information gathered from visioning exercises to develop the DEI business case, readiness assessments, and DEI strategic plans and objectives.

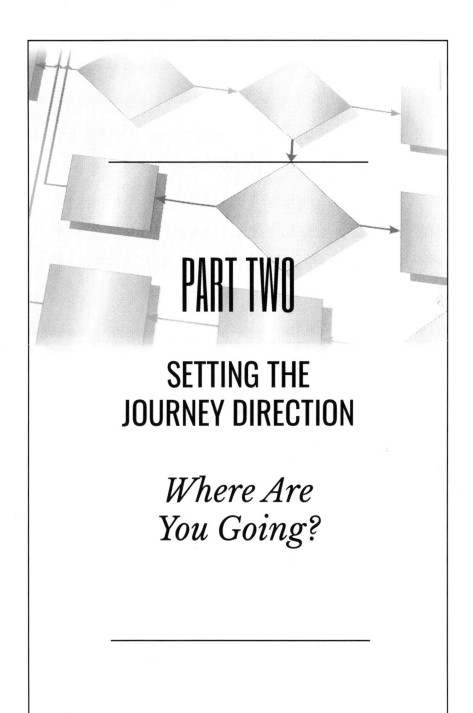

PART TWO

SETTING THE
JOURNEY DIRECTION

*Where Are
You Going?*

LESSON 4
Be Clear About the Vision for DEI

Make sure everyone knows where you are going, why you are going there, and how it will impact them.

"Before you ask the organization to accompany you on the DEI journey, they need to know why they should, where you are taking them, and what they will gain for going along."

Start With "Why"

"If the "why" isn't connected to the business, it is just a nice thing to do, not a key business strategy."

The business case is the reason "why" you are going on the DEI journey.

To establish a DEI business case may sound cliché to some and even cold to others. Focusing on the business side may seem self-serving and not about doing what is right. I have worked with organizations that are uncomfortable connecting DEI to the bottom line. I understand all of that, and I am also sensitive to it.

Our communities are watching with scrutiny. Organizations are right to be careful in how they approach DEI. However, I do not know of any organization or business that can be sustainable without a sound business strategy. DEI must be part of that strategy to be systemic and woven into the culture. Everyone knows any initiative not strategically aligned will die off in time.

Let's talk about what a sound and clear business case is.

According to the Oxford Dictionary, a **business case** is *"a justification for a proposed project or undertaking based on its expected commercial benefit."*

When it comes to DEI, most leaders forget that they are running a business. Therefore, I want to help change that paradigm. By treating DEI like any other key strategy, it becomes a vehicle to:

- Meet your strategic objectives
- Obtain growth in markets
- Live your company values
- Attract top talent
- Make better decisions
- Create innovative ideas and solutions
- Serve your diverse internal and external communities
- Develop better products and services
- Remain competitive and agile

DEVELOPING A SOUND BUSINESS CASE

A sound business case has three main ingredients:

- Relevancy
- Realism
- Meaningfulness

Let's talk about each criterion:

- **Relevancy:** The DEI business case must be relevant to where you are going as a business. The case should show how DEI will help get you there.
- **Realistic:** The DEI business case must be realistic. Everyone must believe that it can be achieved.
- **Meaningfulness:** The DEI business case must make sense to everyone who reads it, supports it, and must carry it out.

"Organizations building DEI cultures separate themselves from those doing diversity by connecting their business case to the overall direction of the organization."

Where Are You Going?

"A clear vision lets everyone know where you are going with DEI. It sounds simple; however, many organizations find articulating it difficult."

A Clear Vision

There are three major benefits to striving for a clear vision. These benefits are:

1. A clear vision allows everyone to know what you are trying to achieve.
2. A clear vision makes it easier for key stakeholders to buy in and understand their roles in its achievement.
3. A clear vision outlines the end goal and a clear image of how success looks, as well as an aspiration for its attainment.

Questions to consider when drafting vision statements might include:

- What problem(s) are we seeking to solve?
- Where are we headed in DEI?
- What would we look like if we achieved our strategic goals in five to ten years?

DEFINE DEI IN THE VISION

What is DEI to you?

When it comes to DEI, definitions are unique to every organization. A common misconception is that your stakeholders and employees understand what your company means in terms of diversity, equity, and inclusion. Therefore, it is important to define each, so everyone understands their purpose in the organization.

Defining Diversity

When defining diversity, it is vital to acknowledge that diversity often means different things to different people. Therefore, it is important to define it carefully. Defining diversity broadly allows everyone in your organization to find themselves in it. Simply said, everyone is diverse. Every employee, every leader, every peer, every customer, and every community member. So, think inclusively.

Yes, White Men Are Diverse!

Many senior leadership teams are largely made up of white males. Often, these leaders do not view themselves as included in diversity as they are implicitly excluded. This is a huge misstep and a disservice to a large segment of your organization. White males must find themselves included in the initiative. If not, they may be hard-pressed to fully support it and feel connected to it. They may even be threatened by it. Therefore, it is important to ensure everyone is included in its definition.

Defining Equity

"Equity is something you measure. It is the glue that holds diversity and inclusion together."

When it comes to equity, many people use equality and equity interchangeably. They are indeed different. Equality is treating everyone equally. Equity is acknowledging barriers that prevent certain groups from equal access. It also includes removing barriers to promote a level playing field.

It is easy to think that treating everyone equally is fair. However, at times, you may have to treat people differently to be fair.

Defining Inclusion

"Inclusion happens when you know your people well enough to leverage their skills, talents, and abilities, and ensure they feel welcome and embraced."

Inclusion is about how you feel in the workplace environment. Therefore, creating inclusion is about building the right environment to tap the diverse talents, ideas, insights, and perspectives. In an inclusive culture, everyone feels the wins, has a common goal, contributes, and knows their role on the team. Answering how you will ensure that everyone feels included, respected, and embraced in your organization is important.

Everyone wants to know how they will fit in. Therefore, be sure to create definitions that help facilitate what it will feel like to every member of your culture.

As you embark on the DEI journey, you must bring everyone along. This means ensuring that your workforce understands why you are embarking on the journey. They also need to understand the vision, where you are headed, and how it will look and feel when you arrive. Therefore, being clear about your vision and definitions, and communicating them, helps get people on board.

CHAPTER SUMMARY
Lesson 4: Be Clear About the Vision for DEI

"Make sure everyone knows where you are going, why you are going there and how it will impact them."

Key Lessons

1. Be sure to establish a business case rationale that is relevant, meaningful, and realistic.

2. Establish an aspirational and clear vision of where you are headed.

3. Do not assume everyone understands what you mean by DEI. They also need to know how it will feel when you arrive.

4. Define diversity broadly, including white males, so everyone finds themselves in the definition.

5. Align your DEI vision with the strategic direction of the organization.

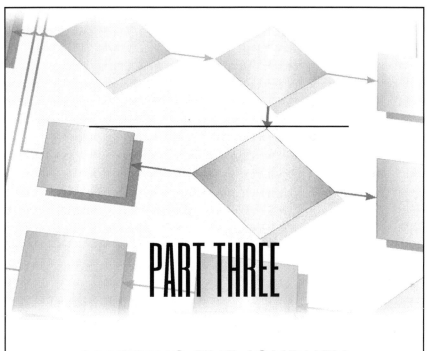

PART THREE

MAPPING THE JOURNEY

*How Do You
Get There?*

Get the Right Leader to Navigate the Journey

Having the right DEI leader who is highly respected, knows the business, and is politically savvy is important to lead the mission.

"If you believe DEI is a key business strategy, don't hand the responsibility to just anyone. Instead, take time to find the right navigator."

Most organizations would never put just anyone in a key senior position, except when it comes to DEI. In my experience, the DEI leadership position is treated like a hot potato; it's passed around until it lands in someone's hands. Usually, that someone has no experience in DEI, culture change, or driving a business strategy. A common pitfall is thinking that anyone can do this job. That is far from the truth. Few leaders are equipped to carry out this task, so it is important to choose wisely.

As with any critical business strategy, choosing the appropriate leader to guide you is critical. The same is true for DEI. The DEI journey will require someone with strategic expertise. Therefore, it takes someone with a strong strategic approach to cultural change, political savviness, and extensive leadership and influence.

The first step to selecting the right navigator is to consider selecting a senior leader who is a peer to other senior leaders. A leader who is in charge of key business strategies is recommended. Therefore, the DEI leader should come from the executive-level ranks and report to the CEO or most senior leader. This is important in positioning DEI for success. This ensures the leader understands the business, is strategic and has the respect of other senior leaders. Selecting a senior leader demonstrates the importance and commitment of DEI to the organization. It also ensures that the DEI leader is at the decision-making table, not an afterthought.

Having the DEI leader at the decision-making table allows them the ability to impact business decisions and ensure that DEI is aligned with your strategic direction. It also helps facilitate a trusting partnership with peers and supervisors. When the CEO, or most senior leader, uses the DEI leader like they use the Chief Financial Officer (CFO) or finance executive, then, they are a trusted partner set up for success. Therefore, the ideal DEI leader should be a strategic business partner to senior leadership.

In addition to being a strategic business partner, the DEI leader needs specific competencies to be effective. The recommended competencies are as follows:

- **Business Knowledge:** It is important the DEI leader understands the business, how the organization makes money, and how it operates.
- **Strategic and Visionary Leadership:** The DEI leader should have experience in strategic planning and implementation and the ability to create long-term visions.
- **Change Management:** The DEI leader will help navigate the culture change, which will require significant systemic changes. Therefore, their ability to facilitate the movement from the current to the future state is

important to the journey.

- **Results and Outcomes Driven:** The DEI leader must focus on driving results and outcomes and communicate the link of DEI objectives, goals, and strategies to bottom-line results.

- **Credibility and Respect:** The DEI leader must maintain credibility, influence change, and earn respect through results, relationships, behaviors, and attitudes as they navigate the journey.

- **Openness, Awareness, and Knowledge:** The DEI leader must be open to new ideas, approaches, and preferences and seek to understand others. They must also be self-aware and hungry for knowledge and continuous learning to stay current as communities change.

The DEI Leader Should Be Independent of Human Resources

An important lesson learned from my experience is to refrain from putting the DEI leadership role under human resources. However, many organizations do just that. Placing the DEI leadership role under human resources or making the Chief Human Resources Officer (CHRO) the Chief Diversity Officer (CDO) or DEI leader is common. This is indeed a recipe for doing diversity instead of building a DEI culture.

As a former human resources executive with over two decades of working with CHROs, I can honestly say CHROs are too busy to drive DEI. Most of the CHROs are bogged down with administrative tasks and putting out organizational fires. Their role soon becomes transactional instead of transformational, as required for a DEI leader.

The CHRO role is robust, and the scope of their responsibility is broad. However, to think they have the capacity to navigate the DEI culture journey is a misnomer. This practice often leads to a swamped DEI leader struggling to keep balls in the air. Soon, they find themselves just doing DEI and lacking the capacity to drive systemic change.

Lastly, the human resources department has yet to earn the respect it deserves in organizations. Although human resources departments play a valuable role, most leadership teams position them into transactional paradigms. Therefore, when the human resources department is responsible for DEI, they are rarely at the decision-making table. That hampers change.

The DEI Leader Qualifications Should be Broader than Just Direct DEI Experience and/or Passion

Hiring a leader with strict DEI experience is not enough to drive systemic change. Some of the best DEI leaders come from outside the DEI profession. The DEI leader should understand DEI and its importance to the sustainability and growth of the organization. They should also possess cultural awareness and sensitivity and be open to differences. However, understanding the business, being a respected leader with influence, and having a strategic approach to operations are more important than strict DEI experience.

Strict DEI experience is not the only reason some fall into the position of DEI leader. At times, passion for DEI can get you there. I have run into many good-hearted leaders who demonstrated a passion for DEI by volunteering on a DEI committee, standing up for sensitivity, or expressing DEI concerns. Soon, they are tapped for the role.

Passion for DEI is great for the navigating leader. However, it takes more than passion for navigating the DEI strategy. Look beyond passion to include other qualifications to set up the DEI journey for success.

Don't Take the Easy Way Out by Selecting Someone Due to Demographics, Because You Must Fill the Role or Solve a Personnel Problem.

In addition to looking beyond strict DEI experience, an organization should not fall into the trap of thinking that only people of color, or those from underrepresented groups, should be DEI leaders. Often, I've seen an organization tap the only person of color, or the sole woman on the leadership team, for this responsibility. Often, this person finds themselves with the hot potato and no support.

It is difficult to admit how often I have seen this scenario play out. The person of color or woman is tasked with implementing a DEI strategy often without any resources, budget, or staff—often on top of another full-time position. Soon, they find themselves unable to do the job well. This leads to the lack of credibility often associated with doing DEI. Unfortunately, this also paints a picture that only such a person can do this job or that you are not thinking strategically about the role.

If you are just doing diversity, then anyone can do the job. However, if it is a key business strategy, you must look for the best-qualified person.

Using the DEI role to solve a personnel issue is also problematic when bringing credibility. For example, some organizations use the DEI position to solve performance issues with leaders. At times, the organization may have also found itself in a bind with such a leader. To terminate them could be a political nightmare. Therefore, they find themselves with a leader they cannot remove. So, what do they do? They give them the hot potato and assign them as DEI leader.

Having the right leader in charge of DEI is critical to the journey. Don't assume that anyone can do the job. To earn the respect of the senior leaders responsible for driving the DEI culture, the DEI leader must have their respect and the ability to influence lasting, tangible change through relationships.

If you reach too far down the organization, select a leader for DEI experience and passion, or because they fit a particular demographic, you may find yourself with a leader who is set up to just scratch the surface. Avoid connecting it to HR roles. If you do, they may end up doing diversity instead of building a DEI culture. Instead, hire a leader with the right experience. Give them adequate resources, and you'll see your efforts soar.

CHAPTER SUMMARY
Lesson 5: Get the Right Leader to
Navigate the Journey

"Having the right DEI leader who is highly
respected, knows the business, and is politically
savvy is important to lead the mission."

KEY LESSONS

1. To drive a DEI culture, it requires an understanding of the business, a strategic approach, political savviness, extensive leadership skills, and influence.

2. The leader should be independent of human resources.

3. The leader should be a peer to other C-suite or senior leaders in charge of key business strategies and at the table when decisions are made.

4. Do not take the easy way out by selecting someone due to demographics because you must fill the role or solve a personnel problem.

5. Take time to find the right navigator. Do not look too far down in the organization. This role requires certain competencies to drive the journey forward.

LESSON 6:
Develop a Plan and Structure for DEI

It is difficult to execute and sustain the journey without a plan and structure to drive it forward.

"DEI is a key business strategy. It requires a plan to carry it out. Without one, it is difficult to get everyone on board and moving in the right direction."

Benjamin Franklin is accredited with stating the adage: *"If you fail to plan, you are planning to fail."* That is indeed a lesson learned when it comes to building a DEI culture.

It is difficult to move forward and continue the momentum without a plan. When you fail to plan, it makes it challenging to:

- Communicate what you are trying to achieve
- Determine what resources you will need to achieve results
- Define the behaviors or processes to meet objectives
- Outline what progress looks like and how you will measure it

Many organizations jump into DEI. They implement programs, trainings, and initiatives without aligning them with the organization's strategic direction. This practice makes it difficult to communicate why DEI is important and how it is a key business strategy.

There are many reasons why organizations fail to plan. However, the most common reasons in my experience are because:

- **Planning is not quick.** It is faster to jump in than it is to sit and plan. Planning takes time, and most leadership teams simply don't have time. Their plates are full, and they also want to see immediate progress.

- **Planning is not easy.** Planning requires bringing people together and thinking through objectives, challenges, and goals. This is not always easy for most leadership teams, especially those who work in fast-paced cultures.

- **Planning is not fun.** Implementing DEI celebrations and trainings is more fun than sitting in a room developing a strategic plan. Most of us get more out of seeing a box checked in the name of DEI than we do from taking time to work through strategic alignment.

- **Planning takes skills.** Developing a DEI strategic plan takes knowledge and skills that most teams lack. Many teams do not know how to develop strategies to achieve the goals and a process for tracking them.

Due to many barriers facing organizations, failing to plan is common. However, without one, many organizations struggle to communicate the objectives and keep momentum. Therefore, every DEI journey needs a strategy to move forward.

DEI Strategic Planning

Having a DEI strategic plan pays off when it comes to building an effective DEI culture. According to the McLean & Company, *Moving from Diversity to Inclusion* report, a DEI strategy makes you one and half times more likely to be effective in DEI. The main objective of a DEI plan is to align an organization's behavior with its strategic goals. Therefore, the strategic plan must outline what behaviors will help you meet your objectives if you are building a DEI culture.

The plan also maps out how the behaviors will be acquired, monitored, and enforced. It also outlines resources to meet the objectives. According to Wikipedia, *"A strategy describes how the ends (goals) will be achieved by the means (resources)."*

They go further to describe a strategy as "setting strategic goals, determining actions to achieve the goals, and mobilizing resources to execute the actions."

Therefore, without a strategic plan, it's difficult to communicate the DEI objectives (the why), your goals (the what), and the strategies to get you there (the how).

Points to Consider When Developing the Plan

Don't overpromise: Your objectives must meet your capabilities. It is easy to fall into the trap of promising the world. Make sure you have the resources, time, and support to carry out the objectives or build that into the plan.

Make the timeline achievable: The timeframe must be reasonable. Most strategic plans span three to five years. Don't try to cram a million objectives into a year or two. You will only overwhelm everyone.

Communicate the plan: Nothing is worse than having a plan that no one knows about. The plan is an organizational one that requires everyone to play a role. Therefore, everyone needs to know about it and how they are progressing. So don't keep it a secret.

Create a plan you can live with, but one that is nimble: It is vital to remember strategic plans are not etched in stone. They are guides to help you achieve objectives. They must be reevaluated as things change in the marketplace, communities, labor market, and the organizational climate.

Engage your leaders in the planning: Most effective strategies involve senior leaders in their development. The same is true for DEI. When senior leaders are involved in the process, not only does it ensure it is aligned with strategic objectives, but it also elevates the plan in the eyes of your workforce. Involving senior leaders also helps increase the chance of accountability, achieving realistic goals, and demonstrating commitment.

Visit the plan often: Strategic plans are living documents and should not die on a shelf. They are to be monitored, communicated, and reassessed. They are your guide to systemic culture transformation and a tool to demonstrate commitment and credibility. Plans also provide recognition when goals are accomplished, and progress is made. Don't let them die a slow death through neglect.

Do not give up on the plan too soon: Strategies have both short- and long-term goals. DEI strategies are not different. It takes time to see results, and you will lose support when people see it as a short-term initiative. But, on the other hand, results will come with a plan, confidence, and patience.

Build a DEI Structure to Carry Out the Plan

"Often, when we hear the word infrastructure, we think of roads, airports, and bridges. We seldom think of DEI."

Now that you have your strategy, you must ensure a structure to hold it up and carry it forward. The structure is your roads, airports, and bridges. In most organizations, that structure does not exist. According to Wikipedia, *"There are both hard structures, like facilities, and soft structures, like institutions, that maintain cultural standards."*

Building a DEI structure requires you to focus on the strategic plan (the hard structure) and the operationalization of the plan (the soft structure). Both are critical to driving your plan forward and bringing it to realization.

Organizations often lose steam when it comes to the structural stage. This is when most realize the work, action, and transformation necessary for a DEI culture. It is also when you feel the pain points and where the temptation to convert to doing diversity appears.

Consider Implementing a DEI Governance Structure

A best practice is establishing a governance structure to help develop your plan and help drive it forward. There are many approaches. One shoe does not fit all. Many organizations develop one or more of the following:

- Executive DEI Councils made up of senior leaders
- DEI Councils or Committees made up of front-line employees and middle management
- DEI Committees made up of various employees at various levels
- DEI Advisory Committees/Councils made up of various employees at various levels

Again, organizations may have a variety of structural approaches. However, according to Cornell University IRL School of Management, it is best to have a structure to do the following:

- *Create the DEI strategy and strategic plan.*
- *Connect DEI strategy objectives to business objectives.*
- *Consider practices and processes that impact DEI.*
- *Drive organizational cultural change.*

Support DEI with Adequate Funding and Resources

"DEI is one of the most underfunded and under-resourced strategies in organizations."

Every strategy requires adequate resources to carry it forward. Those resources may come in the form of human capital, financing and funding, materials and tools, outside expertise, and leadership. Dedicated resources allow your DEI strategy to blossom, and accountability keeps people committed. Nothing fizzles out a strategy faster than lack of support. Put your money and resources where your mouth is to see long-term results.

A plan will set the stage to engage key stakeholders, clarify what you hope to achieve, and communicate goals and objectives. A plan will also allow you to align DEI to the organization's overall strategic objectives and ensure accountability. This is critical to sustainability and progress. Set your DEI efforts up for success with a plan and the structure it requires to survive. This is vital to the DEI journey.

CHAPTER SUMMARY
Lesson 6: Develop a Plan and Structure for DEI

*"It is difficult to execute and sustain the journey
without a plan and structure to drive it forward."*

KEY LESSONS

1. Develop a DEI strategic plan in the same format you
   develop your overall strategic plan.

2. Do not overpromise. Make the timeline reasonable. Most
   plans span three to five years.

3. Engage senior leaders in the DEI strategic plan
   development.

4. Develop a DEI structure to uphold and drive the plan.
   A governance structure that fits your organization is a
   best practice.

5. Support your DEI plan with resources. Do not let it fizzle
   or lack credibility without adequate support to keep it
   alive.

Integrate Core Values and Accountability into Everything

To help drive a DEI culture, integrate your values into every policy, procedure, practice, and program. Then, hold everyone accountable.

*"If you don't live your core values,
you can kiss a DEI culture goodbye."*

When I inform clients that they could be on their way to a DEI culture if they lived their values, most have difficulty believing it.

However, your core values are the attitudes, behaviors, and beliefs that guide your culture. Think about the culture you would have if you lived them, not just posted them on the wall. What type of environment would it create? I ask all leadership teams to do this when guiding them on the DEI journey.

Living your values, in most cases, creates a diverse, equitable, and inclusive work environment. That is why over eighty percent of *Fortune 100* companies have them. Leadership teams spend countless hours in retreats and strategy meetings, developing, revising, and approving them. These drafts often make it to marketing departments to ensure they appeal to internal and external communities.

Although companies spend a lot of time developing values, few put as much energy into holding people accountable to them. It is through your values that you reach your DEI goals and objectives. In other words, you reach objectives by turning your values into actions.

Your values are also your roadmap to how you want your workforce to behave. It is your vision for your organization's future. Therefore, choosing the ones you can live with, and those that enhance your organization's climate is essential.

In the 2002 *Harvard Business Review (HBR)* article *Make Your Values Mean Something*, Patrick Lencioni, the author of several books, including *The Five Dysfunctions of a Team*, and founder and president of *The Table Group*, outlines three types of company values.

Lencioni describes these three types as:

- **The Core Values:** *values that are deeply ingrained principles that guide all a company's actions; they serve as its cultural cornerstones.*

- **The Aspirational Values:** *values that a company needs to succeed in the future, but currently lacks.*

- **The Permission-to-Play Values:** *values that reflect the minimum behavioral and social standards required of any employee.*

It is important to understand the difference between the value types to create an environment where people not only live them, but understand them, as well.

Assess Which Values Are Lived Currently and Why

**"The true culture of your organization is based on
the values you live, not the ones you list."**

A common practice I use with leadership teams is to take them through a *Values Assessment*. This exercise is to determine which values they live by currently and why. This helps understand the organization's true culture and how it may impact DEI. The exercise usually involves answering three main questions:

1. What values do you live currently?
2. Why do you live those values?
3. How does living those values impact, enhance, and/or hamper DEI?

This exercise is an eye-opener for most. Providing a looking glass into the true culture and how they truly operate is surprising.

According to the *Harvard Business Review's* 2021 report, *Company Culture Is Everyone's Responsibility*, by Denise Lee Yohn, *"At many organizations, there is a gap between the existing culture and the desired culture needed to support and advance the company's goals and strategies."*

Most teams are surprised when they learn that the values they live currently hamper DEI. Oftentimes, living only some of the values could be barriers to achieving DEI objectives. Also, it becomes clear that even with a lofty values list, often only two or three of them are lived consistently.

It is also important to understand why you live certain values over others. This is important because it reveals what is rewarded and valued by leaders. Often, you will see that the values that are lived reflect the values of the leadership.

Leaders Are Key to Living Your Values and a DEI Culture

*"Leaders are the drivers of the culture. The values
they live create the culture you have."*

Holding leaders accountable for living your values is critical. According to the 2019 culture report, *"The High Cost of a Toxic Workplace Culture: How Culture Impacts the Workforce—and the Bottom Line,"* by the human resources professional association, *Society of Human Resources (SHRM),* seventy-six percent of employees believe that managers set the culture.

The SHRM report also found that thirty-six percent of employees believe their managers do not know how to lead. Forty percent believe managers fail to engage in honest conversations, and fifty-eight percent left jobs because of their manager's impact on the culture.

Lastly, the SHRM culture report also found that it cost U.S. organizations $223 billion due to employee turnover in the last five years. That is a huge cost to organizations when they do not hold leaders accountable to core values.

8 Ways to Put Values into Actions That Everyone May Live

1. **Make sure you have the right ones.** You may have spent a lot of time developing your core values. However, you may benefit from one more review. Determine if they are the right values for your company. Ensure that you can live with them and that they are the ones to drive the culture needed for your strategic objectives.

2. **Treat company values as your behavioral scorecard.** When searching for key metrics to determine how you are progressing, do not overlook values. You must find ways to determine if people, especially leaders, are living them. The values lead to diversity, equity, and inclusion. Living them gives you a better chance of building a DEI culture.

3. **Start with leadership.** Leaders are key to the culture of DEI. Do your leaders live your values? Do you hold them accountable, and do you eliminate those who do not? These difficult questions are critical to a DEI culture. It is also why most struggle with cultural transformations and continuous improvement.

4. **View your values through the DEI lens.** This is another practice I often conduct when I work with organizations. Viewing values through a DEI lens helps determine how they contribute to a DEI culture. This also helps leaders understand how they translate and what it may mean when they transform the culture.

5. **Consider the chronological order of your values.** Most company values are not listed in order of importance. Instead, they are presented as equally important. In other words, they are not ranked. However, it is important to consider that although the leadership may not see them as ranked, human nature usually sees things in chronological order.

    The value you state first is what most will see as the top priority and value. With that in mind, I often encourage leaders to ensure they live up to the first stated value at a minimum. If you don't live up to the first value, the rest do not matter.

6. **Find visible ways to demonstrate your commitment to your values**. Actions speak louder than words. People believe in what you do, not what you say. To transform a culture, you must exhibit visible behaviors that show your internal and external communities that you live and stand behind them.

    You should reward those who live them, and discipline or eliminate those who do not. It is not enough to say it in words. People need to see it in action.

7. **Communicate them often.** Experts state that employees need to hear values communicated from senior leaders up to seven times before they consider them credible. Therefore, find multiple ways and vehicles to get the word out. Providing leader talking points and scheduled communication touch points helps a great deal.

8. **Integrate the values into everything you do.** It is important to weave your core values through every process and procedure to embed them into the culture. Every process that involves or touches employees and customers must be done through your values, including but not limited to: recruiting, hiring, interviewing, onboarding, educating, promoting, terminating, decision making, communicating, collaborating, developing, and servicing.

Hire for the Values You Want, Not the Values You Live

The talent you bring to your organization will either perpetuate the status quo or help transform it into the desired culture. Therefore, it is important not to hire those who fit the current environment.

Instead, select those who possess the values for the DEI future. Communicating, training, and integrating your core values into the hiring process is critical. Be sure to provide training and tools.

Selecting leaders who live the values should also apply to those considered for upward mobility. So often, leaders are promoted for tangible accomplishments. However, if those individuals do not live your values, they often sabotage the transformation to a DEI culture.

Most leaders support and buy into the core values. However, to demonstrate that commitment requires daily proof. Actions speak louder than value statements. Therefore, you must communicate your values often and keep them front of mind. You must also find ways to hold everyone in your organization accountable by integrating them into everything you do.

Remember, people believe in what you do. Connect your efforts with your values, so everyone knows you stand behind your words. Before you know it, you could be well on your way to a DEI culture.

CHAPTER SUMMARY
Lesson 7: Integrate Core Values and Accountability into Everything

"To help drive a DEI culture, integrate your values into every policy, procedure, practice and program. Then, hold everyone accountable."

KEY LESSONS

1. Determine which values you live currently, and the ones you do not. Then, determine why and the impact. This will help understand the barriers to a DEI culture.

2. Hold leaders accountable for living them and be willing to address those who do not.

3. Hire for the values you want. Be sure to consider values in promotion and advancement opportunities.

4. View your values through a DEI lens to see how they translate in a DEI culture.

5. Demonstrate your values every day and integrate them through everything you do.

LESSON 8
Align DEI Training with the DEI Strategy

DEI training should support the DEI strategy. Having a vision and a plan will help align education, development, and learnings to meet the objectives.

"If your workforce doesn't see the connection of DEI training to the overall strategic direction, it becomes another ineffective obligation."

A common mishap is implementing DEI training as a first step on the DEI journey. Unfortunately, many organizations fall into this practice. In fact, according to *Workforce Management*, around $8 billion is spent annually on DEI training. In addition, a 2021 commissioned study conducted by *Hanover Research*, which surveyed 340 finance decision-makers in the United States, Canada, and Mexico, found that eighty-six percent are expanding DEI training budgets.

In the current climate, focusing on DEI training is not surprising. Organizations such as community police departments, government agencies, as well as for-profit and not-for-profit companies are on the DEI educational bandwagon. Having an educated workforce on DEI helps create a more inclusive, respectful, and equitable workplace. However, although training and education are essential, it has their proper place on the journey.

The proper place for training is after you have a DEI strategy. The strategy must be communicated to your workforce, making the connection between the training and objectives. It is tempting to put the cart before the horse. Even organizations taking a strategic approach are often tempted to start with training before implementing a DEI strategy and plan.

The rush has to do with an urgency to do something now. The rush is also a reactive approach to external or internal pressures. Many are looking to check the box to show they are committed. DEI training is sometimes mandated, or there may be DEI issues at play. However, I caution organizations to wait. Having a vision and a strategic plan will help align learnings to meet your objectives.

The Training and Educational Impact on Organizations

It is helpful to think about why you are implementing DEI training in the first place. If you are like most, you are implementing training as a developmental way to improve your overall effectiveness. However, training should also help educate your workforce on how you want them to behave, work together, communicate, and lead to meet goals and objectives.

Training and development are proven ways to increase productivity, collaboration, leadership, coaching, employee morale, engagement, customer service, products, and communication. In addition, training is critical to meeting organizational goals, strategic targets, employee mobility, and sustainability. Therefore, aligning your training and educational programs around the skills, knowledge and abilities you need to meet those objectives makes sense.

Communication is Key to Training & Education Buy-In

Most organizations assign DEI training without informing their workforce about the goal. As a result, employees are often left in the dark about how the training will impact the organization. They are also unaware of the skills you are building. Communication is critical to ensuring DEI training is well received by all. Key training points to convey should include the following:

- Why DEI training and education are important to your organization
- How the DEI training aligns with the strategic objectives of the organization
- Your key objectives for the training and why
- The outcomes you are hoping to achieve, i.e., skills, behaviors, and awareness
- How you determined the training topics, learning objectives, and facilitated methods
- How training was assigned by organizational roles, levels, and positions, and why
- What training was assigned by organizational roles, levels, and positions, and why
- How training will be delivered and the timeframe
- How you will measure the impact and effectiveness
- How employees may provide feedback, suggestions, and ideas

Without communicating a plan, DEI training may become another requirement that no one understands or cares about.

Align DEI Training with Your Business Goals to Enhance Effectiveness

Unless DEI training is aligned with meeting business goals, it is likely to be ineffective. That is what a 2011 study led by University of Arizona sociologist Alexandra Kalev found. Kalev's study, involving 31 years of data from 830 U.S. workplaces, discovered when DEI trainings are mandatory and not connected to business goals, they were less effective than voluntary trainings aligned with the business.

Your DEI vision and strategic plan will help define the required skills, education, and knowledge to achieve objectives and build the desired DEI culture. Therefore, you must start with your plan and align the training to it.

Align Training with Core Values

Do not assume your workforce knows how to live your values and what behaviors are expected of them. Therefore, educating your workforce about core values is another good place to start. This sounds elementary; however, I am amazed that many companies never train for them.

When it comes to educating for values, start with leaders. They must understand how to role model them, and this takes skills. The training should help build those skills. Education on core values should also include the total workforce and key stakeholders.

Assign Training According to Organizational Roles

In building a DEI culture, everyone contributes based on the roles they serve. In other words, each role has a significant impact on the culture. Therefore, training should be specific to those roles. They also need to understand what DEI means, how the organization defines it, and the connection to the organization's priorities. Therefore, be sure to equip everyone with basic information to build a foundation of understanding and awareness.

Here are examples of suggested DEI knowledge, skills, and abilities by organizational roles;

CEO and Senior/Executive Management

The senior executive team has the most significant impact on the DEI culture. Therefore, their training must equip them accordingly. They require specific skills and knowledge in building and leading a DEI culture. They also require exceptional cultural awareness of themselves and others.

Human Resources Personnel

Human resources also hold a significant role in building the DEI culture. Their role will require a paradigm shift. They require skills to transition from a common transactional role to a transformational one. HR also needs skills to coach leaders for a DEI culture and build structures to hold leaders accountable for how they lead—not solely on outcomes and results.

Supervisors/Middle Management

Middle management is critical to the DEI culture. They are closest to employees. Managers require skills that engage employees and demonstrate inclusive leadership. Effective communication is essential to these leaders. According to the *Society of Human Resources Management (SHRM)*, *"Lack of communication between managers and workers is a leading contributor to the cultural issues facing many organizations."*

Line-Level Employees and Staff

Employees also hold roles that contribute to an inclusive and collaborative culture. Therefore, they require knowledge, skills, and abilities on how to treat each other with respect and dignity. They also need to know how to collaborate and interact with different groups. Aligning their behaviors with the core values should also be incorporated.

CHAPTER SUMMARY
Lesson 8: Align DEI Training with the DEI Strategy

*"DEI training should support the DEI strategy.
Having a vision and a plan will help align education,
development, and learnings to meet the objectives."*

KEY LESSONS

1. Do not rush to training and education without a plan.

2. Make the connection of DEI training to the strategic
   direction and business goals of the organization clear.

3. Be sure to provide all employees with basic DEI training
   to build a foundation of awareness and understanding.

4. Build the core values into the training to obtain the
   culture you desire.

5. Do not ram everyone into the same training by using
   the one-shoe-fits-all approach. Instead, assign and
   design training based on roles and responsibilities.

LESSON 9
Engage Everyone in the DEI Journey

Create opportunities for employees to be part of the solution, process, and experience to promote a DEI culture.

"When it comes to DEI, leaders often see employees as the body that tells them what they are doing wrong. However, they should be considered the body who tells them what to do right."

"Teamwork makes the dream work" is a famous quote from American author and leadership coach, John C. Maxwell. Although Maxwell was focused on leadership when he said that quote, the same rings true for DEI. It takes everyone to make it work. It is the people who breathe life into it. Therefore, find ways to allow your employees to have a stake in its attainment.

Employees have to live, perform and excel in your culture. It is through their performance that your organization excels. Therefore, they can be an asset to keep you informed of your progress on the DEI journey. Serving as an internal resource, employees may let you know how far or how close you are to your goals.

Employees may also provide ideas, strategies, and approaches to keep you on track. Therefore, the more opportunities to provide input, the more likely you are to build a culture where they may be successful. If used constructively, your employees provide a multitude of avenues to keep DEI moving forward. So, find various ways to engage them. The following are examples to consider.

Start By Keeping Employees in the Loop

Feeling *"left out of the loop"* is a common complaint I hear from employee focus group participants. Having facilitated several such groups over the years, I cannot tell you how many times I have heard this concern. In a DEI culture, employees are included, considered, and tapped. Therefore, engaging them must include consistent communication. Informed employees are significant assets to a DEI culture.

A missed opportunity is the failure to bring employees along in the process. Nothing is more disengaging than a workforce in the dark about your DEI efforts, progress, and commitments. Changes in culture must be communicated to all involved. In the absence of information, anecdotes, misconceptions, and suspicions fill the void. Therefore, start your employee engagement with information and keep the lines of communication open at all times.

Organizations often fail to communicate effectively for fear of being scrutinized by their workforce. I see this often in organizations that lack trust. They avoid transparency because the leaders do not trust employees and vice versa. You must break through that and create loops of information. They need to be informed to be part of the solution.

See the Employee Workforce as Internal Focus Groups

Your employee workforce is a valuable resource that is often underutilized. If given the opportunity, they will let you know if you are moving in the right direction. They know what is working, what you are doing well, and what can make it better. Therefore, take full advantage by providing ways for continuous feedback. Below are a few employee contribution opportunities to consider:

- Internal focus groups
- Project teams
- Planning committees
- Feedback channels
- Unifying units
- Temperature checks and balances
- Innovation and idea generators

Build a Trusting Relationship to Increase Employee Resourcefulness

"When employees trust you, they give more, are more honest, and become a better resource."

Trust is the foundation of all constructive relationships. Therefore, you must focus on building trust with your employees. In my experience, an effective way to build it is to get to know your employees well. Create opportunities to interact with them as much as possible. This will allow you to engage, hear their concerns and build a rapport. Trust is built when people feel understood, when voices are heard, and when they believe you care.

Encourage your leaders to also build a trusting relationship with their teams. They should use inclusive leadership skills to increase trust and equity. They must get to know all of their team members and engage with them often. Frequent communication is critical. They must be equipped with these skills, and ways to hold them accountable must be built into their performance evaluations.

Remember, trust is built over time. However, it can be destroyed overnight. Therefore, every action, decision, and practice you take, and the ones you do not, should consider whether it will enhance trust or weaken it.

Sanction Employee/Business Resource Groups

Many organizations have employee resource groups (ERGs), also known as affinity groups. These are groups where passionate employees network and discuss DEI. They also promote workplace inclusion, support diversity recruitment, and provide opportunities for professional development. These groups are useful in giving employees a forum to connect with like-minded colleagues. They are also a beneficial way in engaging employees as a DEI resource.

To obtain the most value from ERGs, consider ERGs not solely employee-focused but business-focused. When they serve both employees and the business, they may serve as a vehicle to drive DEI as a key business strategy.

As business resource groups, they may align their missions with the organization's strategic priorities. In this capacity, such groups have been instrumental in finding new market niches, attracting top talent, and enhancing customer service. They also have led to designing innovative products and better service to diverse communities.

Hold Everyone Accountable for DEI Success

Everyone in your organization should be held accountable for DEI. This accountability should be clear, tracked, and in writing based on roles and levels in the organization. If people do not know their role or how they contribute to DEI's success, it is difficult to get support through actions to move the agenda.

Holding employees accountable to the DEI culture starts with incorporating your values into performance evaluations. You must also communicate behavioral expectations and how they link to the DEI strategic plan and overall strategic objectives.

Show Engagement to Keep Them Engaged

Employees need to know you are engaged in DEI before they engage. Therefore, it is important to consistently demonstrate how you support DEI. Be open about your journey, your vision, and your learnings. Let them know you hear them and that you are keeping a pulse on the culture. Ask them to help keep you accountable. If your engagement fizzles, so will theirs. So, keep up the momentum, the commitment, and the drive. They will not let you down.

Be sure to engage everyone on the DEI journey. It takes the entire village to make an effective DEI culture. However, be sure to not only engage them, but keep them in the loop. They must know where you are going and where you are on the journey. Once they are informed, they may serve as a resource to keep tabs on your progress. They may also find solutions to overcome challenges. Do not leave them out. They are partners in your DEI success.

CHAPTER SUMMARY
Lesson 9: Engage Everyone in the DEI Journey

"Create opportunities for employees to be
part of the solution, process, and experience
to promote a DEI culture."

KEY LESSONS

1. Keep the workforce informed along the way. They must be in the loop to be part of the solution.

2. Create many opportunities to build trust and engage employees in the DEI journey. Incorporating continuous feedback channels, as well as specific project teams and committees, allow employees to contribute.

3. Consider transitioning employee focus groups to business focus groups. You will not only provide networking opportunities, but get employees involved in aligning DEI efforts with overall strategic objectives.

4. Hold everyone accountable for a DEI culture. Outline expectations and communicate them so that all know what it takes to build and sustain a DEI culture and what role they play.

5. Show engagement to get engagement. Nothing fizzles out the commitment to DEI more than when a CEO lacks it.

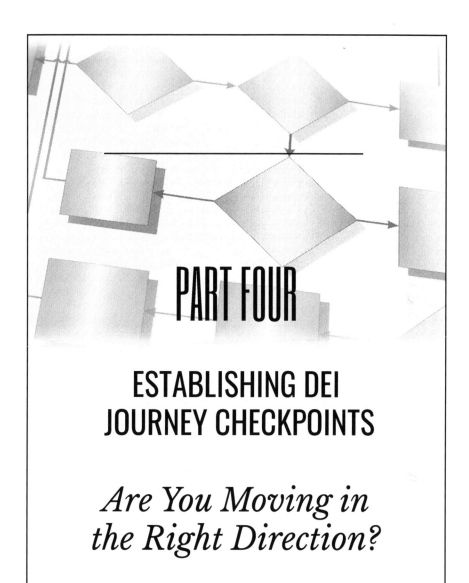

PART FOUR

ESTABLISHING DEI JOURNEY CHECKPOINTS

Are You Moving in the Right Direction?

Track, Measure, and Communicate Progress

When measuring success, tie metrics to the behaviors and actions that lead to progress and communicate how you are doing.

"To get the right things done for a DEI culture, measure what you have to do, not the outcomes you hope to achieve. Then, communicate progress."

How Do We Know We Are Successful?

This is a question I would expect to receive from a CEO. Most of you are results-oriented, and you measure your success by accomplishments. You understand the importance of meeting goals and objectives. You are concerned about making a difference and demonstrating that difference in tangible ways. Therefore, knowing if you are successful is important. However, before we discuss how to determine success, it is crucial to understand a few things:

1. You Must Accept the Truth About DEI Metrics and Success

The truth is that DEI success only comes with consistency, accountability, and targeted efforts. However, it does not come overnight. Therefore, when it comes to DEI, you must be patient.
Changing a culture takes time and is difficult to measure. Change happens slowly and in small shifts. That is what makes it challenging to measure. Therefore, if you are not measuring the small changes, it is easy to miss the progress.

Also, much of the progress in DEI is qualitative, not quantitative, which is also difficult to measure. This reality frustrates most CEOs and often leads to selecting the wrong metrics. When you are eager to see progress, it is tempting to select metrics where movement is visible and immediate. Metrics such as representation, number of hires, turnover percentages, etc., become the go-to metrics for doing diversity. However, focusing solely on these metrics may not provide adequate measures of success in culture transformation.

2. You Cannot Get There Without Doing the Work

To understand what it takes to achieve success, I often look to legendary football coach Vince Lombardi's statement, *"The only place success comes before work is in the dictionary."*

Lombardi, known for leading the Green Bay Packers to five NFL Championships and winning the first two Super Bowls, knew what it took to succeed. Therefore, his words resonate when I think of DEI's success.

It will take work to succeed in DEI. So, to track progress, your metrics should also measure the work it takes to succeed. In other words, determine what work you must do to meet the objectives. Then, link your metrics to it.

3. You Will Need to Identify Your Leading and Lagging Indicators

"Start with the lagging indicators (the outcomes you want) and work backward to the leading indicators (what it takes to get there)."

Many CEOs are familiar with leading and lagging indicators regarding performance measurement. For example, world-renowned business and technology thought leader, Bernard Marr, describes them this way, *"A leading indicator looks forward at future outcomes and events. A lagging indicator looks back at whether the intended result was achieved."*

It is helpful to identify your lagging indicators first. Start with the outcomes will help determine what it takes to get there and ultimately guide you to the leading indicators. Once you define the leading indicators, find ways to measure them. These metrics are what you track on your road to success.

The leading indicators (the work) determine success. Although it is challenging to measure, the work is where the rubber meets the road in building a DEI culture. Therefore, you will have to resist a natural tendency to track (the outcomes) or lagging indicators. If not, you will find it difficult to determine if you are building a culture for long-term success.

Now that we got those important points out of the way, let us explore ways to measure success.

Link Metrics to Behaviors and Actions That Drive Outcomes

An old adage says, *"What gets measured gets done."* It is an adage because it is true. The same applies to DEI. Applying metrics to the actions, behaviors, and commitments that drive DEI will ensure you get what needs to be done. This is the only way to set up for long-term success. When you focus solely on outcomes, you may see progress. However, understanding what led to the progress is most important.

In my experience, most executive teams are skeptical about measuring DEI success. They have never experienced the positive impact of a DEI culture on organizational performance, the bottom line, or strategic objectives. They may see the impact from an external perspective on products and services. However, they won't see the impact from an internal cultural perspective.

There are many reasons why the impact of a DEI culture has not been visible to leadership teams, including:

- Lack of a formal DEI strategic plan with targeted goals and objectives
- Failure to select metrics that impact and measure actions, behaviors and commitments
- Patience and faith for the process to work

This is when a strategic plan with goals and objectives comes in handy. It can serve as the template for your metrics. It is the plan that will drive your metrics. Set your goals to align with your DEI objectives and what you hope to achieve with your DEI efforts.

Focus on How You Play

"It is how you play the game, not whether you win, that changes a culture."

In order to make progress, you must change your thinking from winning the game to how to effectively play the game. This is another adage many of us heard growing up. When you are building a culture, you want to encourage certain behaviors that enhance your chances of winning and create an environment for success. This is a paradigm shift required on the DEI journey.

Many organizations measure performance based on an increase in diversity. Many also tie this metric to bonuses and compensation of leaders. In fact, tying diversity to compensation is considered a best practice in DEI. However, this often leads to behaviors that do not enhance a DEI culture, but often hamper it instead.

Leaders will do what they are rewarded for doing. For example, if you reward them for bringing in more diverse hires, they will do that. However, how they accomplish the goal is important. In my experience, how they accomplish it often hurts DEI.

When the outcome is more important than how you get there, leaders struggle to find the right way to make it happen. As a result, most become frustrated and burdened by the diversity goal. Others are often clueless about how to achieve it. Below are comments I have heard from leaders struggling to meet this objective:

"How will I meet the goal when there are not enough diverse candidates out there?"

"I am now biased against white males when it comes to hiring."

"Do I have to still hire a diverse candidate even if they are not qualified?"

"Are we lowering our standards to hire more diversity?"

"It will take too much time to find more diversity, and I do not have time to wait."

"This is a numbers or quotas game."

"What do I tell other leaders about why we have to hire diverse candidates?"

"What about the non-diverse employees in the succession pipeline? Will they still have a career here?"

"What if our clients have a problem with a diverse leader?"

"How do I talk to a diverse candidate, and what do I say if they ask me about diversity?"

When the focus is solely on the outcome and not how you get there, leaders will take the path of least resistance. That path is to hire diversity no matter what. This leads to perceived quotas, the belief that unqualified candidates are hired over more qualified ones, and that new hires are just "diversity hires." This does not help build a DEI culture.

You must focus on equitable and inclusive behaviors and explain why these behaviors are important to what you are building. This will make it clear that your overall objective is to increase diversity. However, how you achieve it is as important as the goal itself.

Identifying the Right Metrics to Drive Change

When driving change, you must focus on the behaviors that will make the change happen. Therefore, measuring how many diverse hires you made last year does not tell you whether your culture is moving in the right direction. Only the behaviors that got you there will reveal your true success.

The right metrics to drive progress must be aligned with DEI behaviors. These DEI behaviors are the leading indicators. This does not mean you do not also track lagging indicators. It just means that the leading ones tell you if you are making progress in culture change.

Let's look at the human resources research and advisory firm *McClean & Company's 2021 HR Trends Report* to provide some direction. In surveying 850 business professionals, they identified the following actions that lead to DEI effectiveness:

- *Providing DEI training*
- *Embedding inclusive behaviors into values*
- *Evaluating inclusive leadership behaviors in performance appraisals*

These actions provide a good start to identifying the right leading metrics. Let's walk through an example using my **Outcomes, Actions, and Metrics (OAM) Model** to identify potential leading indicator metrics that will drive DEI progress.

Outcomes, Actions, and Metrics (OAM) Model to Measure DEI Progress OAM MODEL™

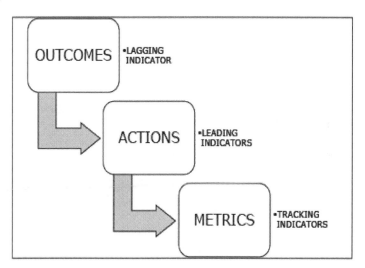

The **OAM Model™** is my acronym for *Outcomes, Actions and Metrics.*

1.   Outcomes

First, determine the outcomes you wish to achieve (the Lagging Indicators).

2.   Actions

Second, determine how to achieve the outcomes through actions, behaviors, and structures. This means identifying the actions (the Leading Indicators) required to achieve the desired outcomes.

3. Metrics

Third, determine how you will measure the actions, behaviors, and structural changes (the Leading Indicators) and tie metrics to them. These are what you track to ensure progress to a DEI culture.

Let us walk through this example and the steps in FIGURE 1.:

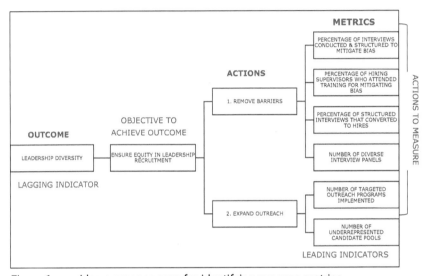

Figure 1. provides a process map for identifying success metrics.

Step 1.

Identify the Outcome: Leadership Diversity (Lagging Indicator)

Objective To Achieve the Outcome: Ensuring Equity in Leadership Recruitment

Step 2.

Identify the Actions to Achieve Outcome:

1. Remove Barriers

2. Expand Outreach

Step 3.

Identify the Metrics (tied to actions, these become the success metrics):

Action 1. Remove Barriers Metrics (Leading Indicators)

- Percentage of Interviews Conducted & Structured to Mitigate Bias
- Percentage of Hiring Supervisors Who Attended Training for Mitigating Bias
- Percentage of Structured Interviews That Converted to Hires
- Number of Diverse Interview Panels

Action 2. Expand Outreach Metrics (Leading Indicators)

- Number of Targeted Outreach Programs Implemented
- Number of Underrepresented Candidate Pools

Other Metrics to Leverage

When investigating relevant metrics, looking at your collected data is good practice. This includes metrics and data such as:

- Equal employment opportunity and affirmative action data reports
- Equal employment opportunity, discrimination, and grievance claims

- Employee complaints
- Cultural, climate audits, exit surveys, and assessments
- Focus group feedback, customer surveys, management and employee evaluations
- Workforce data such as turnover, hires, and terminations, attendance reports, succession plans

The Diversity Primer, Diversity Best Practices Report, outlines the following metrics to consider when determining the return on investment (ROI) of diversity and inclusion:

- *Level of participation in the firm's diversity and inclusion vision formulation*
- *Number of underrepresented employees in formal mentoring programs who get promoted*
- *Percentage of diversity objectives aligned with key strategic business objectives that are tied to bonus and compensation systems*
- *Representation on the board of directors*
- *Overall organizational climate and culture ratings and their effects on all represented groups*

Engage Employees in Determining Leading and Lagging Metrics

When it comes to determining leading and lagging indicators, employees are also a good resource. They are astute at articulating what it will take to meet your outcomes. Navigating through your policies, procedures, and practices, they are familiar with your current culture's barriers, behaviors, and challenges.

Facilitating employee focus groups is also an excellent way of finding adequate metrics. Employee resource groups, DEI committees, and councils may be another resource. Also, consider sharing your metrics once established with these groups to get feedback or additional suggestions.

DEI success only comes after the work. Therefore, it requires consistency, accountability, and targeted efforts. This does not happen overnight. You must resist the temptation to seek quick fixes and progress. Building a culture involves changing behaviors and instituting actions to drive the change. This is where the progress is and where your metrics should align. Measure what needs to get done to ensure it does.

CHAPTER SUMMARY
Lesson 10: Track, Measure, and Communicate Progress

"When measuring success, tie metrics to the behaviors and actions that lead to progress and communicate how you are doing."

KEY LESSONS

1. Accept the truth about DEI metrics. Change is difficult to measure, and it is incremental. Therefore, have patience and determination to stay the course.

2. DEI success comes only with consistency, accountability, targeted efforts—and work!

3. Applying metrics to the actions, behaviors, and commitments that drive DEI will ensure you get done what needs to get done. This is the only way to set up for long-term success.

4. Leaders will do what they are rewarded for doing. For example, if you reward them for bringing in more hires, they will do that. However, how they accomplish the goal is important.

5. When it comes to determining leading and lagging indicators, employees may be a good resource. Consider sharing metrics once established to get feedback or additional suggestions.

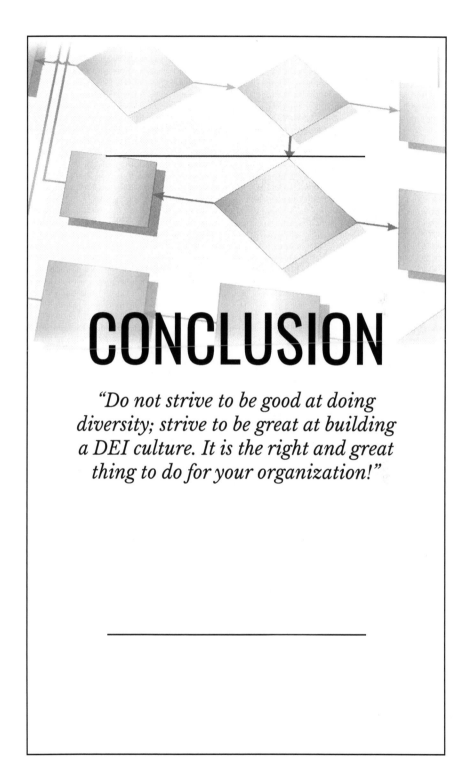

CONCLUSION

"Do not strive to be good at doing diversity; strive to be great at building a DEI culture. It is the right and great thing to do for your organization!"

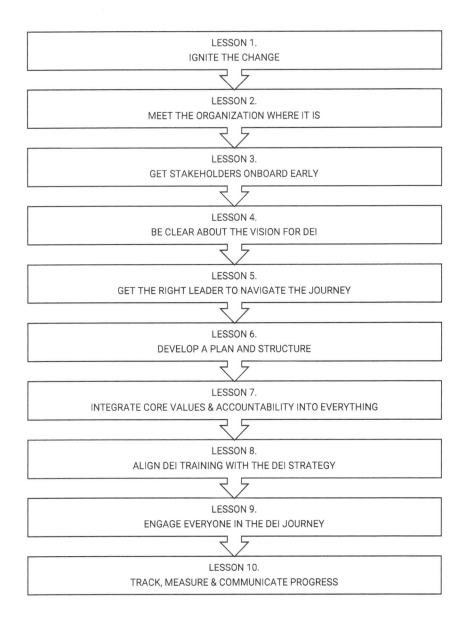

As we end our DEI culture journey, I want to thank you for stepping up to be part of the great. That is top-down commitment to building a culture of DEI.

Diversity, equity, and inclusion are mainly about change. However, the most important change starts with you. As CEO, you must ignite the change and demonstrate your top-down commitment every day. Your actions, decisions, and what you accept from leaders will serve as your report card and credibility. Therefore, you and only you can ensure a DEI culture.

Beginning the DEI cultural journey can be a daunting endeavor. You may feel confused about where to start. You may wonder if you are on the right track and if success is around the corner.

Those are common questions and concerns of great leaders. This is a big job. However, you would not be here if you were not up to the challenge.

Leaders like you are passionate about your people, your organization, and the communities you serve. Therefore, do not disservice them by moving too fast, failing to prepare them, or not providing adequate skills and awareness. You must meet them where they are. Be sure to get help, if needed, including an inclusive coach.

Engaging your leaders and key stakeholders early is critical. They must be part of the vision, the strategy, and the solution. They are also key to driving the vision forward and the credibility of the journey itself. You should also be clear about where you are taking your organization. Before your workforce gets on board, they need to understand why they should and what they stand to gain.

Do not keep your people out of the loop. You must be open and transparent. You must build trust, communicate often, and listen to understand. When you engage everyone, all can be part of the solution. Also, be sure to be inclusive and not make this about certain groups. Everyone must be part of DEI to make it work.

Now that you understand this is a big job, you must have a robust navigator. This is not a responsibility that just anyone can do. It requires strategic planning, change management, business acumen, and, most importantly, respect from peers. Avoid reaching down in the organization for this role and aligning it with human resources. This role is part of the credibility and top-down commitment. Therefore, take time to find the right leader and set them up for success.

The right leader will also serve as a strategic partner to you and other senior leaders. You must trust them enough to confide in them and provide a seat at the decision-making table. The right DEI leader will be instrumental in the development of your DEI strategy, goals, and objectives. They will be vital to engaging other senior leaders in the process, as well as ensuring accountability to it.

Human resources (HR) will also play a major role. Regarding DEI, HR will have to revamp its role in developing new policies, practices, and procedures. Mainly, they will help turn values into behaviors. They may also make paradigm shifts to help measure leaders' performance in living those values and aligning training with the DEI vision.

As we wrap up our time together, I want to emphasize the importance of engaging your employees on this journey. Be sure to seek various ways to allow their contributions, ideas, feedback, and input to be heard and implemented. They know what it takes to navigate through your organization. They also know the barriers and opportunities for improvement. Failing to take advantage of their insight and trust will be a missed opportunity. They are your trusted partner in this work.

Measuring success is also important. However, how you achieve success is more important than success itself. For sustainability, it is critical to ensure that you are building a culture with behaviors and actions that support DEI. Therefore, tying your metrics to actions that promote desired outcomes is the focus. This means progress will be difficult to see at first. However, DEI is a commitment to patience and faith. If you build it, they will come.

In closing, it is essential to remember that this is indeed a journey. You will have setbacks. You will get dirty, and you may have detours. However, what makes you great is that your top-down commitment never diminishes. This is why you stand out from the good and what makes you part of the great. Better yet, it is what makes your organization greater!

Thank you for the opportunity to partner with you on this journey. It has been a pleasure, and I hope to engage again soon.

Now go out, ignite the change, and be great (for your organization)!

Your guide and friend,

APPENDIX

Quotes to Ponder
by Jocelyn Giangrande

"Do not strive to be good at doing diversity; strive to be great at building a DEI culture."

"DEI is more than something you do. It is who you are."

"A transparent organization focuses on three important words: communication, honesty, and trust."

"It is easy to tell if an organization stands a chance of sustaining the DEI journey by observing the CEO."

"I never met a CEO who has not asked, "What's the biggest mistake when launching a DEI journey?" My answer is always the same: failure to assess if your organization is ready."

"Your leadership must be invested in the DEI journey from the onset, or you will have an uphill battle."

"To get the buy-in of your leadership, don't tell them why DEI is a business imperative; instead, have them tell you."

"Before you ask your organization to accompany you on the DEI journey, they need to know why they should, where you are taking them, and what they will gain for going along."

"If the "why" isn't connected to the business, it is just a nice thing to do; it's not a key business strategy."

"Organizations building DEI cultures separate themselves from those doing diversity by connecting their business case to the overall direction of the organization."

"A clear vision lets everyone know where you are going with DEI. It sounds simple; however, many organizations find articulating it difficult."

"Equity is something you measure. It is the glue that holds diversity and inclusion together."

"Inclusion is when you know your people enough to leverage their skills, talents, and abilities, and ensure they feel welcome and embraced."

"If you believe DEI is a key business strategy, don't hand the responsibility to just anyone. Instead, take time to find the right navigator."

"DEI is a key business strategy. It requires a plan to carry it out. Without one, it is difficult to get everyone on board and moving in the right direction."

"Often, when we hear the word infrastructure, we think of roads, airports, and bridges. We seldom think of DEI."

"DEI is one of the most underfunded and under-resourced strategies in organizations."

"If you don't live your core values, you can kiss a DEI culture goodbye."

"The true culture of your organization is based on the values you live, not the ones you list."

"Leaders are the drivers of the culture. The values they live create the culture."

"If your workforce doesn't see the connection of DEI training to the overall strategic direction, it becomes another ineffective obligation."

"When it comes to DEI, leaders often see employees as the body that tells them what they are doing wrong. However, they should be considered the body who tells them what to do right."

"When employees trust you, they give more, are more honest, and become a better resource."

"To obtain a systemic DEI culture, you must have systemic metrics throughout the entire operation."

"Start with the lagging indicators (the outcomes you want) and work backward to the leading indicators (what it takes to get there)."

"To get the right things done for a DEI culture, measure what you have to do, not the outcomes you hope to achieve."

"It is how you play the game, not whether you win, that changes a culture."

"To get the right things done for a DEI culture, measure what you have to do, not the outcomes you hope to achieve. Then, communicate progress."

Bibliography

1. "Fundamentals of Diversity Initiatives", Cornell ILR School, Management Programs, (2008): p.31 DV 221 Section 4

2. Hiatt, Jeffrey M. ADKAR, How to Implement Successful Change in our Personal Lives and Professional Careers, Loveland, CO: Prosci Learning Center Publications, 2006.

3. Society of Human Resources Management (SHRM). "Strategic Diversity, Equity, and Inclusion Management Plan Development Guide." (2022).

4. Texas A&M University, "Culture."

5. Wakeman, Dave. "3 Steps to Align Project and Strategy." Projectmanager.com. Sep 23, 2015

6. Diversity Best Practices, Diversity Primer, June 1, (2010).

7. Wikipedia: "A strategy describes how the ends (goals) will be achieved by the means (resources)."

8. Collis, David J., Rukstad, Michael G. "Can You Say What Your Strategy is?" Harvard Business Review, April, (2008)

9. Lencioni, Patrick. "Make Your Values Mean Something." Harvard Business Review, (2002)

10. "The Ten Things We Know to be True." Google.com

11. Society of Human Resources (SHRM). "The High Cost of a Toxic Workplace Culture: How Culture Impacts the Workforce—and the Bottom Line." Culture Report, (2019)

12. Yohn, Denise Lee. "Company Culture Is Everyone's Responsibility" Harvard Business Review, (2021)

13. Livingston, Robert. "How to Promote Racial Equity in the Workplace." Harvard Kennedy School Center for Public Leadership. Harvard Business Review (2020): 65-72.

14. Rinne, April. "A Futurist's Guide to Preparing Your Company for Constant Change." Harvard Business Review, (2021): September 22.

15. Chugh, Dolly. The Person You Mean to Be; How Good People Fight Bias. Harper Collins Publishers (2018).

16. Saska, Sarah. Feminuity.com

17. Vedanta, Shankar. "Most Diversity Training Ineffective, Study Finds." Washington Post, January 20, 2008.

18. Simmons Assoc. of Amber, PA and Bristol, UK/Cornell ILR School

19. Heskett, James. "WHAT DO YOU THINK? How Do We Make Sure the Right People End Up with Power in Organizations?." 04 OCT (2021).

20. "Top 5 Priorities for HR Leaders in 2022 Actionable and objective advice to tackle top HR challenges." Gartner for HR, (2022).

21. Smith, Christie and Turner, Stephanie, PhD. "The Radical Transformation of Diversity and Inclusion the Millennial Influence." Deloitte University

22. Leadership Center for Inclusion Report, Deloitte University Leadership Center for Inclusion, Deloitte Consulting LLP, (2015).

23. York, Duston. "Leaders; This is What More Communication Should Look Like." Fast Company, (2022).

24. "Moving From Diversity to Inclusion, McLean & Company, (2021)

25. "HR Trends Report." McClean & Company, (2021).

26. "The ROI of Diversity and Inclusion, Diversity Primer." Diversity Best Practices; Chapter 2: (2010).

27. Marr, Bernard. "What Is a Leading and A Lagging Indicator? And Why You Need to Understand the Difference. Benardmarr.com. (2016).

28. "Evaluating the Impact of Diversity on Organizational Performance." The Diversity Scorecard, (2004).

29. Dobbin, Frank, Kaley, Alexander, Kim, Soohan. "You Can't Always Get What You Need: Organizational Determinants of Diversity Programs." American Sociological Review 76 (3):386. (2011).

30. McCarthy, Niall. "America's Best Employers for Diversity In 2020." Forbes, Jan 22. (2020)

31. Robinson, Phil. A., Field of Dreams, Universal Pictures, (1989).

About the Author

With a track record of over 25 years of building award-winning inclusive cultures that attract, engage, develop and retain talent, *Jocelyn Giangrande* is a nationally known Cornell University certified diversity expert who knows the right questions to ask and has the courage to challenge leaders of all calibers.

Known for her strategic approach to cultural transformations, shaping diversity visions, and leading the strategic direction of DEI initiatives, Giangrande has partnered with over one hundred organizations on their DEI efforts. Focused on an integrated approach, her consultations, seminars, and trainings are implemented nationally, where her thought-provoking DEI Executive Strategy Retreats are named "culturally transformational."

C-Suite leaders and key stakeholders buy-in, positioning DEI as a business strategy, and strategic alignment with bottom-line results is her specialty. Taking the mystery out of implementing a DEI strategy, Giangrande has a passion and track record of helping stakeholders sequence cutting-edge initiatives that promote compelling visions, sustainability, and accountability.

Jocelyn resides in Michigan with her husband, millennial son, and adopted cats, Hektor and Rousseau.

OTHER WORKS BY JOCELYN GIANGRANDE

*What's In Your Sandwich? 10 Surefire Ingredients
for Career Success*

*What's In Your Sandwich? 7 Savvy Ingredients to
Supercharge Your Confidence*

WEBINARS AND PRESENTATIONS

- *If You're Human, You're Biased: How Our Biases Impact Decisions, Perceptions, and Interactions*
- *DEI for 21st Century Leadership*
- *Leap to Inclusion: How to Become an Inclusive Leader*
- *Through Actions and Results*
- *Communication for a DEI Culture*
- *DEI as a Business Strategy*
- *Understanding Generational Diversity*

Giangrande is known for her thought-provoking keynote presentations, transformational executive DEI retreats as well as leadership development boot camps for women through her SASHE Career Academy for Women (SCAW).

CONNECT WITH JOCELYN
online - www.jocelyngiangrande.com

Made in the USA
Columbia, SC
21 December 2022

74781362R00078